WITHDRAWN FROM
TSC LIBRARY

Rethinking Liberal Equality

Also by Andrew Levine

The Politics of Autonomy: A Kantian Reading of Rousseau's Social Contract
Liberal Democracy: A Critique of Its Theory
Arguing for Socialism: Theoretical Considerations
The End of the State: Rousseau, Marx, Communism
Reconstructing Marxism: Essays on Explanation and the Theory of History
  (co-authored with Erik Olin Wright and Elliott Sober)
The State and Its Critics, vols. 1 and 2 (editor)
The General Will: Rousseau, Marx, Communism

Rethinking Liberal Equality

From a "Utopian" Point of View

ANDREW LEVINE

Cornell University Press   ITHACA AND LONDON

Copyright © 1998 by Cornell University

All rights reserved. Except for brief quotations in a review, this book, or parts thereof, must not be reproduced in any form without permission in writing from the publisher. For information, address Cornell University Press, Sage House, 512 East State Street, Ithaca, New York 14850.

First published 1998 by Cornell University Press

Printed in the United States of America

Levine, Andrew, b. 1944
    Rethinking liberal equality : from a "utopian" point of view / Andrew Levine.
        p.   cm.
    Includes bibliographical references and index.
    ISBN 0-8014-3543-9 (alk. paper).
    1. Equality.   2. Liberalism.   3. Democracy.   I. Title.
JC575.L626   1998
323.42—DC21   98-6790

Cornell University Press strives to use environmentally responsible suppliers and materials to the fullest extent possible in the publishing of its books. Such materials include vegetable-based, low-VOC inks and acid-free papers that are recycled, totally chlorine-free, or partly composed of nonwood fibers.

Cloth printing   10 9 8 7 6 5 4 3 2 1

Contents

Preface

Because it is a discipline without scientific pretensions, political philosophy has never been very constrained by matters of fact. But the real world of
politics impinges on political philosophy nevertheless. Thus the major political
transformations of the past quarter century have had significant philosophical
effects. Indeed, the early 1970s now appear to have been a watershed. The economic expansion that followed the end of the Second World War in all the advanced capitalist countries came to an end around that time, to be replaced by a
period of slow decline. Actually existing socialist regimes entered a period of
prolonged economic and political stagnation culminating eventually in their
demise. And the so-called Third World began to splinter apart: a few countries
achieved a measure of unanticipated economic success, the rest sank deeper into
misery. These momentous changes have resonated throughout the entire political culture. There can be little doubt that they account, in part, for the decline
of the historical Left, almost to the point of extinction, and for the resurgence
of pro-market and antistate ideologies. These phenomena, in turn, have
affected political philosophy profoundly.

On the surface, however, academic political philosophy appears to have
changed very little. In 1971 John Rawls's *A Theory of Justice* was published.
That masterpiece exercises an enormous influence over political philosophy to
this day. The appearance in 1993 of *Political Liberalism,* a redacted collection of
Rawls's essays written in the preceding decade and a half, has brought Rawlsian
concerns even more into the foreground. Needless to say, Rawls's focus has
evolved over the years. Thus *A Theory of Justice* is much less concerned, say,
with cultural diversity and other "facts of pluralism" than *Political Liberalism* is.
But the overall constancy of Rawls's philosophical vision and the nearly hege-
monic influence of his work in so many areas of political philosophy can make

it seem that the discipline has evolved hardly at all in the past quarter century. Those of us who, on balance, regret the way that recent history has affected political philosophy therefore find ourselves complaining both that so little has changed in the past twenty-five years and also that so much has changed for the worse.

On balance, however, it is plain that the Rawlsian turn has been a godsend—especially for egalitarians. More than any other factor, Rawlsian liberalism has kept alive and even breathed new life into an egalitarian vision that, until quite recently, animated a significant political constituency, but now no longer does. It has done so, however, by celebrating some of the institutional arrangements that have superintended the rightward, anti-egalitarian drift in real world politics. This is why I, an unreconstructed egalitarian of the old school, am ambivalent about the current state of academic political philosophy. What follows is an effort to think through this ambivalence and, so far as possible, to resolve it.

With some exceptions (concentrated mainly in Chapters 4 and 5), the topics I address are central to the concerns of political philosophers who have taken the Rawlsian turn—the majority of political philosophers today. But the claims I advance are often at odds with views that are emblematic of the strain of liberal theory they have produced. Thus I favor a form of liberalism that owes more to John Stuart Mill than to Rawls, and I endorse a vision of democracy and community based on some non- or extraliberal ideas of Jean-Jacques Rousseau and Karl Marx. In fact, the position I ultimately defend is not strictly liberal at all. What follows, however, should not unduly disturb open-minded proponents of the kind of liberalism I propose to rethink. As followers of Hegel might say, my aim is to *incorporate* this strain of liberal theory, liberal egalitarianism, along with several of the positions it *negates*, into a new *synthesis*. Of course, it will be impossible here to do more than sketch what I have in mind. The supersession of liberal egalitarianism is a daunting project. Its successful execution can only be the work of many, and the philosophical community nowadays is indifferent, if not hostile, to such an endeavor. But the pendulum is sure to swing back; real-world conditions will see to it. For now, it is worthwhile, I believe, to struggle against the current, even at the risk of appearing antiquated or utopian. Otherwise, some deeply important implications of the egalitarian idea may fall out of sight, rendering their eventual reconstruction all the more difficult. Thus my aim is to show how liberalism, refracted through the work of Rawls and philosophers influenced by him, points the way toward a political philosophy *beyond* its own conceptual horizons. It does so neither intentionally nor self-consciously. But it does so nevertheless.

It is a tenet of Rawls's "political liberalism" that everyone "reasonable" can in principle be brought to support an "overlapping consensus" favoring liberal institutional arrangements. I take issue with some aspects of this view (in Chapter 3), but I agree that liberal theoretical convictions, properly conceived, are more nearly ubiquitous than was widely assumed just a decade or so ago. What follows is not, in the main, a political tract intended to persuade lapsed egalitarians to resume the cause or potential egalitarians to take it up. What follows is, rather, an investigation of the forms and limits of one currently prominent kind of liberal theory, and of what that theory might become, were it successfully joined to some ideas of Rousseauian and Marxian provenance. Even so, I do hope to convince adherents of the broad consensus on values that motivates liberal egalitarians and many others that, despite all that has happened in recent years, the supraliberal vision of the historical Left remains eminently defensible. If this smacks of pouring old wine into new bottles, so be it. The old wine, suitably filtered, is as good as it ever was, and the new bottles are better than the old ones ever were.

I expect that my focus on recent academic political philosophy will disconcert at least a few readers who would otherwise be inclined to support my conclusions. They will find what follows too concerned with current preoccupations and too little focused on traditional left-wing ideas, in short, not "old-fashioned" enough. To them, I would say that liberal political philosophy, as it has developed in the past quarter century, has become indispensable for theorizing some of the values the Left has always advanced. When the Left revives politically, as it eventually must, given the persistence of its reasons for being, there will be no going back to ways of thinking that preceded the Rawlsian turn.

I fear, however, that there will be other readers, a far greater number, who will find what follows hopelessly out of date. They will consider it unconscionable in a "postmodern" age to remain mired in traditional liberal or Rousseauian or Marxian ways of thinking. I should alert readers who might expect to find liberal equality rethought here in a postmodern "register" that they will be disappointed. I will not belabor the point, but I trust that my allergy to "discourses" bearing the prefix "post-" is not so much a personal idiosyncrasy as a rational response to some patently unfortunate developments in the prevailing intellectual climate. I have in mind a certain tendency toward conceptual relativism and, correspondingly, a de facto abandonment of some of the norms of rational argumentation. It is fortunate, therefore, that academic philosophy generally, including political philosophy, has so far remained largely outside the postmodernist ambit. As will become apparent, there are important conceptual affinities joining egalitarian positions with long-standing "modernist" forms of political theory. This fact is a condition for the possibility of conceiving an egalitarian vision that is genuinely supraliberal in content.

I describe this vision as "utopian," but I trust that the reader will understand that the emphasis is on the scare quotes. Strictly speaking, "utopian" suggests institutional arrangements that are impossible to realize under *feasible* real-world conditions. But insofar as the reflections that follow depend on the feasibility of transforming people's dispositions and circumstances, there is, I believe, nothing literally utopian about what I shall say. I appreciate the fact that few readers today will be disposed to agree with me, and I regret that it is simply not possible to assuage their doubts satisfactorily. When positions like the one I develop are faulted for being utopian, philosophical speculations alone can hardly abrogate the charge. It is not at all clear that a more empirically focused inquiry could either. What evidence there is that bears on the issues in contention here is too equivocal to advance the discussion one way or another. I intend the scare quotes to underscore this situation. Now and for the foreseeable future, no one is in a position to say with confidence just how "utopian" it is reasonable to be. I can only hope to make the reader see that my "utopianism" is at least as plausible as the "realism" that has come to dominate contemporary thinking. My hope is that this posture is salutary as well. I would venture that of all the ways that the political culture has changed for the worse in the past quarter century, the one that is most insidious—and perhaps also most detrimental to efforts to change the world for the better—is the apparently inexorable rise of political pessimism and its consequence: a revolution of diminished expectations throughout the remnants of the political Left.

I am grateful to the Institute for Research in the Humanities at the University of Wisconsin–Madison and to the Wisconsin Alumni Research Fund for financial support during the early stages of this project. Harry Brighouse, David Estlund, Daniel Hausman, and Sarah Marchand generously provided me with written comments on various drafts of this book. Special thanks also to Richard Arneson, John Baker, John Broome, Debra Satz, Elliott Sober, and Erik Wright; and to the many other friends, colleagues, and students, too numerous to mention, with whom I have discussed the issues treated here. Chapter 1 draws extensively on an article I published in *Economics and Philosophy* 11, no. 2 (October 1995) called "Fairness to Idleness: Is There (or Ought There to Be) a Right Not to Work?" I am grateful to the editors of that journal for permission to reprint substantial portions of that article, and also to their anonymous reviewers for some very useful criticisms. I now believe that the conclusions I drew there are stronger than my arguments support. Accordingly, Chapter 1 defends a slightly weaker claim than its ancestor does. Finally, I offer special thanks to Alison Shonkwiler of Cornell University Press for seeing this project through to completion.

ANDREW LEVINE

Madison, Wisconsin

Rethinking Liberal Equality

Introduction

Political arguments and ideas exist in particular historical contexts. Political philosophers, however, like philosophers generally, are inclined to engage ideas as such, not as historical artifacts. This approach is probably indispensable for advancing philosophical understanding. But it can also lead philosophical reflection astray. To guard against this possibility, self-awareness is indispensable. I will therefore begin with some observations about the historical context of the positions I will defend.

It is fair to observe that of the major political ideologies, the familiar "isms" that flourished, commingled, and vied with one another throughout modern political history, only one, liberalism, has survived to the end of what Eric Hobsbawm has aptly called the Short Twentieth Century.[1] Readers who are not current with political philosophy may find this contention odd, especially if they understand the word "liberal" in the way that has become commonplace in the United States. They will protest that conservatism is also flourishing and that it has, in fact, all but defeated liberalism politically. They are right, of course, that in the United States and elsewhere, political movements identified with conservatism are currently ascendant. But we should not be misled by the varieties of meanings that attach to the words "liberal" and "conservative," nor should we mistake labels for political philosophies. In the United States, "liberal" designates the left wing and *conservative* the right wing of the mainstream political

---

[1] See Hobsbawm 1994. The term designates the years extending from the outbreak of World War I in 1914 to the collapse of the USSR in 1991, a period which already appears to form a coherent historical period. In Hobsbawm's periodization, the Short Twentieth Century succeeded the Long Nineteenth Century, which began with the American and French Revolutions (1776, 1789) and lasted until the First World War.

ı.[2] What liberalism is will be at issue throughout what follows, espe-
-, ın Chapter 3. But whatever we finally decide, it is plain that contemporary
political usage is distinct from, though generally related to, philosophical understandings of the term. In any case, it is as a political philosophy (or family of
political philosophies) that liberalism is effectively assumed across the existing
political spectrum.

In describing real-world political orientations, I will use the words "left" and
"right" with confidence that readers will understand what I have in mind. It
should be noted, however, that these terms have no fixed meaning. Left and
right are relational concepts; left is defined in contrast to right, and vice versa.
Thus political parties or movements that everyone understands to be on the
Left have their own left and right wings, as do movements and parties acknowledged by all to be on the political Right. I will use these terms in a way
that assumes a fairly definite, though always evolving, reference, one that everyone has come to accept in the years since 1789, when the more radical delegates
to the French National Assembly seated themselves to the left of the presiding
officer. Thus except where otherwise indicated, "Left" and "Right" will designate positions on an idealized political spectrum, approximated in varying degrees in most political cultures and in the "collective consciousness" of virtually
everyone who thinks about political affairs.

It would hardly be possible, nor should it be necessary, to spell out the programs and causes that have motivated the Left and the Right, so conceived, for
more than two hundred years. It will suffice to observe that, in general, the
main ideas in consideration here—democracy, socialism, and, of course, equality—are left-wing ideas, historically and conceptually.[3] In recent years, proponents of these ideas have increasingly gravitated towards liberalism and have
even come to represent themselves as liberals.[4] Thus, in the present conjunc-

---

[2] This usage has become less standard than it used to be. Nowadays, many Americans on the left
of the mainstream spectrum prefer to represent themselves as *progressives*—partly because "liberal"
has become a term of reproach in some sectors of the population, and partly because they disagree
with some long-standing liberal policy prescriptions.

[3] The nature and extent of the Left's commitment to these causes, however, is clouded by the
historical experience of the Left in power in the former Soviet Union and elsewhere. But at least in
words and also to some extent in deeds, even the most tyrannical Left regimes have continued to
endorse democracy, socialism, and equality. Perhaps they were only attempting cynically to legitimate their own power, even as they acted in contravention of these ideals. Even so, the deference
they accorded democracy, socialism, and equality attests to the continuing power of these ideas
over the popular imagination. Ultimately, political philosophers cannot abstain from reflecting
upon the consequences of implementing what they defend. But the sad and ultimately self-
defeating experience of the official Left in power in the Short Twentieth Century has so little to do
with the aspirations of the historical Left that it would be wildly premature to conclude anything
on the basis of this evidence alone.

[4] See, for example, John Roemer's attempt (1994) to identify socialist aspirations with liberal
egalitarian aims.

ture, would-be continuators of the political traditions of the historical Left are effectively and sometimes self-consciously left-wing liberals, just as the continuators of the historical Right have become, self-consciously or not, right-wing liberals. I believe that this turn of events impoverishes political thinking. I also believe that philosophical reflection can remedy this unhappy situation, at least in part.

Having voiced this view, however, I would repeat what I claimed in the Preface: that under the aegis of recent liberal theory, important philosophical advances have been made. No one today can think constructively about equality or democracy or even socialism without taking recent work in liberal theory into account. What follows therefore engages liberalism directly and from within. There is no better way and arguably no other way at the present time to *rethink* equality. I would venture that there is no better strategy for reinvigorating the socialist tradition in political theory than by grappling philosophically with liberalism, and particularly with *liberal* egalitarianism.

It used to be widely believed that socialism represented a continuation of liberalism, not an alternative to it.[5] What follows supports this conviction. In its defense, I will, as noted, make use of the Hegelian metaphor of "supersession" (*Aufhebung*) or, as I shall sometimes say, of going *beyond*. I am not entirely comfortable with this language. It invites obscurantism. Even so, it is suggestive. To go beyond something is not to reject it but to incorporate it—along with its opposite, its negation—into a higher unity. I know of no more apt way to express what I want to say about the relation between liberal equality and what I will call "democratic equality," the idea I will ultimately defend.

Contemporary liberal philosophy is, of course, the work of many. But as I have already remarked, there is one figure who has shaped the nature and direction of liberal theory in recent years more decisively than anyone else—John Rawls. Rawls's writings on distributive justice and political legitimacy constitute the immediate context for what will follow because liberal egalitarianism is, in large part, a creature of Rawlsian moral and political philosophy. Nevertheless, I will only occasionally focus directly on Rawls's express views. This stance is partly tactical: Rawlsian liberalism is a subtle and shifting target, comprised of resources rich enough to address virtually any reasonable criticism—though not, I will contend, always able to accommodate them satisfactorily. To focus directly on Rawls's actual positions is therefore to risk entanglements in

[5] This was the dominant view in the pre–World War I Second International (1889–1914), the period Leszek Kolakowski (1978, vol. 2) has called Marxism's Golden Age. Social democrats, as all Marxists called themselves in those days, considered *social* democracy the successor to liberal democracy. The same conviction was shared by many non-Marxist socialists in both the nineteenth and twentieth centuries, and by many (non-Marxist) social democrats to this day. For a particularly lucid and influential account, see Tawney 1931.

debates that are sure to draw attention away from the larger picture. There is a strategic reason as well: liberal egalitarianism is more than just Rawlsian moral and political philosophy, and liberal egalitarianism is not the only part of the liberal tradition that egalitarians can fruitfully put to use. My claim, then, is not quite that Rawlsian liberalism is ripe for supersession, but that there exists a strain of liberal doctrine—some of it comprised of Rawls's express views, some of it Rawlsian in spirit but opposed to the letter of Rawls's own positions, and some of it compatible with liberal egalitarian convictions but drawn from pre-Rawlsian forms of liberal theory—that defenders of democratic equality must eventually supersede.

When I invoke the idea of *neutrality,* therefore (as I will especially in Chapters 1 and 3), what I have in mind, though Rawlsian in spirit, is not quite in accord with the letter of Rawls's recent work.[6] The same is true for *political liberalism,* the topic of Chapter 3. "Political liberalism" is coming increasingly to designate Rawls's account of political legitimacy, in much the way that "justice as fairness" nowadays names Rawls's theory of justice. My use of "political liberalism" will be somewhat more expansive, as I will explain in due course. I am aware of the danger that readers schooled in Rawls's writings may be misled. But I think the benefits of using language in accessible, nonidiosyncratic ways—and also of distancing the relevant strain of liberal theory from Rawls's account of it—outweigh the costs of possible misunderstandings.

What earlier liberalisms sometimes obscured and recent liberalism makes clear is the very deep conceptual connection joining liberty, officially liberalism's principal concern, with equality. Rawls and liberals influenced by him are not the only ones to see a connection.[7] But nowhere is the link so cogently represented as it is in Rawls's work. Equality, refracted through this prism, will be my point of departure. I will argue ultimately for a *supraliberal egalitarianism,* an egalitarianism *beyond* liberal understandings. From the standpoint of distributive justice, the hallmark of the supraliberal purchase on equality is a relaxation of long-standing views about the connection between what an individual does or is and what that individual ought, as a matter of justice, to receive. I will argue in Chapter 1 that liberal egalitarianism contains conceptual resources that already warrant a very substantial and largely unacknowledged dissociation of contribution from distribution. In subsequent chapters, I will go on to show how supraliberal egalitarianism carries this dissociation further—to the point where egalitarian aims effectively supersede the purview of theories of (distributive) justice altogether. I will argue, in other words, that the egalitarian's distinctive commitment to the moral equality of persons, to what I shall call "deep

---

[6] For some reasons why, see Rawls 1993, 190–95.

[7] See, for example, the account of "equaliberty" in Balibar 1994 and the exchange between Rawls (1995) and Jürgen Habermas (1995).

equality," has implications for social and political life that transcend the usual understanding of egalitarian concerns. My purpose, then, is not only to defend more radically egalitarian distributions than liberal egalitarianism is able to support. I also want to explore some connections between egalitarianism and other political ideas—with democracy, above all. Because democratic and egalitarian theory effectively intersect in ways that I will go on to examine, I call the idea of equality I ultimately defend *democratic* (in contrast to liberal) equality. We will see too that democratic equality has implications for *community,* for our understanding of ourselves as social beings and our relations to others. It will emerge, finally, that the vision of ideal social and political arrangements that democratic equality implies points the way toward a revival of socialist theory as well.

The existence of a socialist alternative to mainstream liberal ways of thinking used to be uncontroversial. Not long ago, too, hardly anyone would have considered liberal political philosophy a likely basis for egalitarian theory. Indeed, the very idea of a liberal egalitarianism might almost have seemed an oxymoron. But the Rawlsian turn has shattered these received understandings. It has made connections between liberalism and egalitarianism plain for all to see. With the recent eclipse of socialist theory, *liberal* egalitarianism has become the most important and arguably even the only live *theoretical* expression of egalitarian aspirations in the world today. Nevertheless, the idea that egalitarianism and liberalism are at odds does contain a kernel of truth. So too, I will argue, does the related conviction that there exists a properly socialist alternative to liberal positions, one that better articulates egalitarian aspirations than any liberalism can.

Liberal and democratic egalitarianism part ways most evidently in their respective construals of community. I will seldom focus directly on community in the pages that follow, but I will directly fault the liberal view. My complaints, however, are not those of contemporary communitarians.[8] For political philosophers today, "communitarianism" suggests a line of criticism that impugns the purported universality of recent and traditional liberal theory. Communitarians claim that Rawls and other liberals employ a false and misleading concept of the person, that they improperly abstract individuals away from the social contexts that shape their respective identities. An adequate theory of justice, the argument goes, must be a theory for real people, not for idealized, featureless selves. Thus, communitarians claim, liberalism misrepresents the essential historicity of human life. Communitarian challenges to mainstream liberalism have subsided in recent years, in part because Rawls and others have demonstrated convincingly that what is sound in the communitarians' complaint does not in fact damage the aspects of liberal theory that it purports to

---

[8] See, among others, Unger 1975; Sandel 1982; MacIntyre 1981; Barber 1984.

upset.[9] In any case, I will not engage the literature on communitarianism here because my quarrel with recent liberalism is not theirs. In my view, liberals ultimately go wrong in conceiving human societies as *collections* of discrete individuals.[10] I will propose instead that for many purposes it is better to construe societies as integral wholes, freely constituted, but irreducible to their constituent parts. This idea is implicit in Rousseau's account of political authority. Rousseau arrived at it by reflecting on what he called the "general will," which he contrasted with particular or private wills. I will argue that the notion of generality implicit in this conception is crucial for the fullest possible (but still defensible) theoretical expression of the egalitarian project. Thus there is a sense in which my criticism of recent liberalism is the opposite of the communitarians'. They fault liberalism for its inattention to individuals' particularities, for its universalistic pretensions. I will argue that the liberal understanding of community is insufficiently general in its perspective, that it is not, as it were, universalistic enough.

As Rousseau's account of the general will suggests, the condition for the possibility of a supraliberal egalitarianism, as for liberal egalitarianism, is what Hegel (1807) called the "moral vision of the world." From the first intimations of "the moral point of view," generality—construed as impartiality or agent neutrality— has been the defining feature of moral deliberation and its extensions to normative theories of social, political, and economic arrangements. Thus the Golden Rule tells us to do unto others as we would have others do unto ourselves—to adopt, in other words, a deliberative standpoint that treats our own interests and those of other moral agents impartially. It is essentially this thought that Kant's categorical imperative articulates when it instructs us to act only on maxims that we could will to be universal laws. Similarly, it is because it would have us deliberate in an agent-neutral way, from no particular agent's perspective, that utilitarianism is a moral theory, in contrast to nonmoral theories of deliberation that recommend straightforward individual utility maximizing.

[9] See Rawls 1993; also Gutmann 1985; Kymlicka 1989. Less thoroughly dispatched are similar charges leveled by feminist writers who maintain that liberals fail to accord proper attention to *gendered* identities. This reproach, however, has more to do with Rawlsian liberalism's neglect of issues having to do with justice within the family than with its allegedly damaging abstractness. See, for example, Nedelsky 1989; Okin 1989.

[10] In Levine 1993, I call this view "atomic individualism." For the ancient atomists, (indivisible) atoms were the fundamental constituents of matter; everything material was built up from them. These atoms, moreover, bore only *external relations* to one another. Thus their relational properties were always contingent; they could fail to obtain and the atom would remain the *same* entity. Whatever is *essentially* true of a particular atom is therefore nonrelational. Atomic individualism pictures human communities analogously. Individuals, the fundamental constituents of human societies, stand in determinate relations to one another. But their relational properties are nonessential.

Impartiality does not by itself imply that all human beings are members of the moral community. This understanding of the scope of impartial deliberation is a distinctively modern idea. Neither does a commitment to impartiality tell us when moral deliberation is appropriate. However, it is plain to all modern thinkers, committed as all are to taking individual interests as their point of departure, that the moral point of view is appropriate when the aim is to justify social, political, and economic arrangements.[11] This is so because in order to persuade others, one must offer reasons they can recognize as legitimate. Agent-specific reasons will generally be compelling only to particular agents. Agent-neutral reasons appeal to agents as such or at least to agents insofar as they are susceptible to being moved by reasons.

Impartiality implies that, as moral agents—and perhaps only in this respect—members of the moral community are equal. Impartiality therefore follows from a deeper commitment to the *moral equality of persons*. Thus it is not as surprising as it may at first appear that, as Amartya Sen has suggested, "every normative theory . . . that has at all stood the test of time seems to demand equality of something—something that is regarded as particularly important in that theory."[12] A commitment to equality of something, Sen observes, is evident not only among professed egalitarians but also in the work of philosophers "who are typically seen as having disputed the 'case for equality' or for 'distributive justice'" or who are apparently indifferent to it. Robert Nozick, for example, is a well-known defender of distributions generated by free markets with virtually unqualified private property rights. Since market transactions, in which individuals are free to do almost anything they want with the resources they control, are bound to upset *any* distributional pattern (including those in which everyone has an equal share), they will typically generate distributions that everyone, including Nozick, would regard as inegalitarian.[13] Then, since Nozick thinks that state-mandated redistributions violate infrangible property rights, one might conclude that at least Nozick's political philosophy is in no way egalitarian. But even Nozick demands equality of something, of libertarian rights. Utilitarians, to take another example, are supposed to care only about maximizing utility, not about its distribution. Thus it would seem that they could hardly be egalitarians. But they are egalitarians in Sen's sense, for they insist that in utilitarian calculations each individual should count equally as a bearer of utility.

[11] *Utilitarians* propose that we maximize over individuals' interests; *rights theorists* would have some interests, articulated in rights claims, "trump" other considerations, including utilitarian calculations; *contractarians* would protect individuals' interests by acquiescing only to arrangements that rational individuals, mindful of their interests, could accept. It is fair to say that all distinctively modern political theories appeal to one or another of these justifying strategies (or to some combination of them).

[12] Sen 1992, 12.
[13] Nozick 1974, 160–64.

From this perspective, debates between proponents of different moral theories are disagreements *among egalitarians* about what should be equally distributed, quarrels over the identity of the *egalitarian distribuand*.

The identity of the egalitarian distribuand was indeed a major topic of debate among philosophers throughout the 1980s and beyond.[14] I will comment on this literature in Chapter 2. At this point, I would only note that, for the most part, participants in this debate effectively rule libertarian, utilitarian, and other ostensibly inegalitarian positions out of bounds. I think they are wise to do so, if only to connect their interest in egalitarianism with the historical phenomenon of egalitarian politics; for even if everyone is an egalitarian in Sen's sense, not everyone is an egalitarian in the ordinary political understanding of the term. To accommodate this obvious but important point, I will follow the lead of those who would exclude positions like Nozick's from the egalitarian camp, and I will regard utilitarian objectives as only contingently connected with egalitarian concerns.[15]

Most people today are egalitarians (in the political sense) to some extent. But some are more egalitarian than others. For true egalitarians, equality is the preeminent concern; for the rest, it is a lesser value. Nothing hinges on this difference in degree here. It is worth observing, however, that even the most ardent egalitarians are not for equality exclusively, nor do they always prefer equality to other values with which it may conflict. Thus child rearing in family units (of any imaginable kind) is almost certainly an obstacle in the way of according children fully equal opportunities. But proponents of equal opportunity seldom, if ever, inveigh against family-based child rearing as such. Equality is a *defeasible* standard, an ideal that egalitarians balance against competing values and sometimes even derogate for the sake of other ends. Thus when I speak of egalitarians in the pages that follow, I have in mind egalitarians qua egalitarians. When I engage the question Sen posed—What do egalitarians want?—I will mean, What do they want insofar as they want equality?

Following Rawls (1971), it is widely understood that actual distributions, whether in capitalist market economies or in other imaginable economic systems, are largely undeserved—in consequence of the fact that they depend sub-

[14] What is widely known as "the equality of what?" debate was launched by Sen (1980), before he came to the view that all modern moral, social, and political philosophies are egalitarian. Important contributions to this discussion include, among many others, Dworkin 1981a, 1981b; Arneson 1989; Cohen 1989; and a recent one by Sen himself (1992).

[15] Utilitarianism has egalitarian implications (in the sense in question) whenever it is the case that arranging institutions to accord with utilitarian objectives will, as a matter of fact, require moving toward equality or diminishing inequalities, according to the usual understanding of the term. Utilitarian normative theorizing has often tended toward egalitarianism in this sense, most evidently in classical welfare economics. See Little 1957.

stantially on morally arbitrary factors, on luck in "the natural lottery." But for liberals of all stripes, *free choices* are not arbitrary from a moral point of view. Thus what qualifies an egalitarian position as *liberal* is a dedication to hold individuals responsible for the distributional consequences of what they freely choose to do. Joining this conviction to the claim that other factors affecting individuals' holdings are morally arbitrary, we can conclude that there is at least a prima facie liberal egalitarian case for having distributions reflect the consequences of individuals' choices insofar as they are free—and nothing else. This is not to say that liberal egalitarianism *requires* the nullification of the distributive consequences of morally arbitrary factors. Rawls's Difference Principle is a case in point. It maintains that an unequal distribution of, for example, income is required by justice if, but only if, the inequality enhances the distributive share of the least well off. Thus if the least well off can be made at least as well-off under capitalist market arrangements as they can under alternative economic systems, capitalist markets would be allowable under the Difference Principle, even though they plainly permit individuals to benefit from morally arbitrary factors. This is, in fact, Rawls's view; he believes that capitalism can be just.[16] But liberal egalitarianism does place the burden of proof on anyone who would allow inequalities generated by morally arbitrary factors. It presumes equal distributions just until proven otherwise. This position drives a wedge between facts about what individuals do or are and claims about what they ought as a matter of justice to receive. Thus it goes a long way toward dissociating contribution from distribution. As I have said, my aim will be to push beyond this frontier—to a point where the very focus on distribution itself passes away from the foreground of egalitarian concerns.

Liberal egalitarians generally assume that equality is to be realized through particular distributions of *privately owned* resources. I will begin by following their lead. This assumption will eventually come into question, however. It will become clear that supraliberal egalitarianism is at odds with the unqualified commitment to private property that liberal egalitarians take for granted. This is why rethinking liberal equality bears on socialism. John Roemer (1994) has claimed that what socialists have always wanted, whether they realized it or not, is liberal equality. I will argue, to the contrary, that what egalitarians ought to want is socialism. Of course, strictly speaking, "socialism" designates a form of property relations, and it would be foolish and doctrinaire to want a form of property relations for its own sake. But it does not therefore follow, as Roemer believes, that socialists are or ought to be for socialism only because they hold beliefs about its consequences for liberal equality. Egalitarians want socialism

---

[16] Rawls also believes that socialist economic systems can be just. See Rawls 1971, 258–74.

because it is indispensable for the kind of democracy and community that a commitment to equality implies. Properly conceived, socialism is essential for democratic equality and, therefore, for what egalitarians, even mainstream liberal egalitarians, ultimately want.

I have suggested that we advance toward equality to the degree that we dissociate contribution from distribution, and that liberal egalitarianism does so to a very substantial degree. In Chapter 1, I investigate how radical the liberal egalitarian dissociation of contribution from distribution can be. To this end, I focus on the hard case of voluntary unemployment, arguing that Rawlsian liberalism contains resources that support the idea that even those who freely choose not to participate in the monetized economy have claims on public provision. I argue, in other words, that there are good liberal reasons to support a right not to work, at least in certain circumstances. In defense of this unlikely contention, I employ a concept emblematic of the Rawlsian turn in liberal theory, the idea that public (coercive) institutions ought to be *neutral* with respect to competing conceptions of the good. I also investigate widely shared intuitions about reciprocity and its antonym, *free riding*.

In Chapter 2, I investigate liberal egalitarianism itself. The "equality of what" literature is my point of departure. My aim, however, is not so much to intervene into that still lingering debate as to exhibit some of its central features and its generally unacknowledged assumptions. In this context, I begin to raise questions about the connections between forms of property and the implementation of egalitarian aims, and I elaborate on some reflections, broached in Chapter 1, on the implications of varying levels of affluence for justice and equality.

Chapters 1 and 2 comprise a sustained reflection on liberal equality. Chapters 3 and 4 engage more directly political aspects of recent and traditional liberal theory. But they also extend the investigations that precede them. To rethink liberal equality, I maintain, it is necessary to put some fundamental aspects of liberalism generally in question.

In Chapter 3, I examine "political liberalism" in Rawls's version and also generically. Political liberals seek to justify liberal constitutional arrangements on grounds that proponents of *reasonable* "comprehensive doctrines" can support. Thus they aim to sever the ties that have traditionally bound liberal political philosophy to underlying moral philosophies. I argue in favor of bringing moral philosophy back in. I show, first, that there is less at stake in the contrast between political liberalism and some of its ancestor doctrines than meets the eye and, second, that insofar as political liberalism really is different, it is less hospitable to egalitarian aspirations than some of its rivals. The principal difference between political liberalism and the form of liberal theory I favor, *instrumental* liberalism, is political—not in the Rawlsian sense that contrasts with moral philosophical, but in the ordinary sense of the term. Political liberalism blocks the supersession of liberal horizons in ways that instrumental liberalism does not. I argue too that although liberals, including political liberals, can fail to be liberal egalitarians and vice versa, the impulse that motivates liberalism also motivates egalitarianism. The conclusion I therefore draw is that the politics of political liberalism, because it is an obstacle in the way of democratic equality, impedes not just egalitarian objectives but liberal aims as well.

To supersede liberal equality, it is necessary, I contend, to supersede liberal democracy too. In Chapter 4, accordingly, I focus sympathetically but also critically on liberal democratic theory. My aim is to investigate the prospects for what I have called supraliberal democracy, a theory and practice *beyond* liberal democracy. To this end, I maintain that liberal concerns can be satisfactorily addressed through the radical democratization of the public realm. I enlist elements of Rousseauian political philosophy in support of this claim. But I also fault Rousseau for failing to accord due weight to the transformative potentialities of liberal institutions themselves and to their continuing importance as the process of radical democratization proceeds. The arguments I offer in support of these contentions depend, in part, on predictions about the consequences that democratic and liberal institutional arrangements have for the characters of individuals living under democratic and liberal institutional arrangements.

Because there is almost no historical experience of radical democracy, I am obliged, like Rousseau, to defend a cautious optimism about the transformative potentialities of democratic participation in a generally speculative way. I venture that, even so, the "utopian" case for the beneficial effects of radical democracy is as plausible as the more pessimistic view of democracy that prevails today. In contrast, we do know a great deal about life under generally liberal regimes. It is fair to say that the available information supports the claims I advance for the transformative effects of liberal institutions. But in this case, too, I rely more on speculation than on historical analysis to defend the contention that liberal institutions promote liberal character development. No matter how much life under liberalism has already transformed people's dispositions, the idea that liberal safeguards will always be fragile in the face of human nature, and therefore in need of institutional implementation forever, is likely to persist. There is probably no way, in the end, to dissuade the resolutely pessimistic. What data, after all, could convince those who believe the cup to be half empty that it is actually half full? Against the charge that the position I defend is literally utopian, there is therefore nothing to do but advance persuasive, albeit inconclusive, reasons for adopting a more optimistic stance.

Chapter 5 brings together the reflections on liberal equality and liberal and democratic political philosophy developed in the preceding chapters in support of *democratic equality,* an ideal that, as I have said, incorporates but also negates distinctively liberal positions. There are, as noted, deep affinities joining the egalitarian vision implicit in this critique of liberal equality to Marxian communism. I discuss some of these connections directly. But ideas of an extra- or nonliberal provenance, communism included, are not my main focus, even in this chapter. Liberalism and democracy are. My aim, again, is to let the rational core of liberal egalitarianism and also its cognate doctrine, liberal democratic theory, unfold—to the point that liberal political philosophy finds itself transformed into something more congruent with the valuational commitments that motivate it and with the political aspirations that used to drive egalitarian theory and practice.

We will find, in the end, that egalitarian concerns merge with the theory of distributive justice only under historically particular, albeit extremely long-standing, conditions. This is why what egalitarians want ultimately has more to do with democracy, community, and socialism than with justice itself. This conclusion is at odds with the letter and the spirit of liberal social and political philosophy. But despite itself, liberalism—or more precisely the strain of liberal theory I rethink—points the way beyond itself. Egalitarians can do no better than follow its lead.

I

Fairness to Idleness

My aim in this chapter will be to defend a *right not to work* against the charge that its provision would be unjust, and to argue that liberalism, as it has developed in recent years, actually supports such a right. Liberals generally oppose the conclusion I will defend. In doing so, they underestimate the extent to which their own theoretical commitments dissociate contribution from distribution. It will be useful to correct this misapprehension before turning to liberal equality itself.

It is widely agreed that involuntary unemployment is an evil for unemployed individuals, who lose both income and the nonpecuniary benefits of paid employment, and for society, which loses the productive labor that the unemployed are unable to expend. It is nearly as widely agreed that, for the sake of justice or benevolence or social order, there are good reasons for alleviating this evil. Finally, there is little doubt that the evils of involuntary unemployment cannot be adequately addressed in contemporary societies without state intervention—whether through monetary or fiscal policies, cash payments or other subsidies to the unemployed, direct provision of employment by the state, or some combination of these measures. At the same time, hardly anyone would have the state relieve *voluntary* unemployment. It is relevant that the voluntarily unemployed include people of independent wealth, unemployed spouses of working men or women, individuals in the midst of career changes, and others whose situations seem not to warrant concern. But there are also people who prefer idleness to paid employment to such a degree that they are willing to suffer considerable (material) hardships in order to remain without work, individuals who without "relief" would be as badly off as the involuntarily unemployed. Voluntarily unemployed individuals without independent means are rare in our society. But voluntary unemployment is the limiting case of voluntary under-employment, and there are quite a few people who choose to be less employed than they could otherwise be. What are we to make of these idlers?

Do the voluntarily idle, like the involuntarily idle, have a right to state support? Most people would say no. This answer is deeply rooted and long-standing. The Elizabethan Poor Laws, for example, denied public provision to able-bodied adult males, apparently on the grounds that anyone who was able to work but was nevertheless unemployed must have chosen idleness over re-munerative employment and had therefore forfeited claims to relief. Adult women were also excluded from public provision, but for the rather different reason that they were excluded from public life altogether. Women were sup-ported by their husbands or, if unmarried, by their families. Until the nine-teenth century, even as women labored in the productive economy, they were seldom part of the (paid) workforce even in principle—and were therefore, as a matter of logic, neither voluntarily nor involuntarily unemployed or underem-ployed. With the widespread entry of women into the paid labor force, the con-sensus on adult males has carried over to women, despite the fact that women's still largely uncontested role as the primary caretakers of children—and the claims of dependent children for public provision—obscure this point. Thus, voluntarily unemployed primary caretakers of children, almost all of whom are women, are thought to have a claim on public assistance, albeit grudgingly and with social stigmas attached. This aid, however, is intended officially for the children; the children's caretakers benefit only indirectly. To be sure, widows of working men do receive state subsides in most modern welfare states. This "ex-ception that proves the rule" is explained, presumably, by the persistence of the outdated assumption that only male heads of households ought to be family providers.

The intuitions supporting these exclusions from public support are deeply entrenched. To most people it seems obvious that able-bodied individuals in the prime of life who choose not to participate in the monetized economy can-not rightfully demand material support from public agencies. Hence the idea that it would be unjust to provide aid to the voluntarily idle (see Elster 1989a, 215–16).

I shall argue against this view and in support of the claim that despite Rawls's own view to the contrary, Rawlsian liberalism implies support for a right not to work. What follows will fall short of a full-fledged, liberal defense of this right, however. To argue for its provision from a generally Rawlsian perspective, it would be necessary to address proposals for its institutional implementation and to examine the consequences of one or another institutional implementa-tion for economic well-being, freedom, democracy, and other relevant con-cerns. I will not attempt anything of the sort here. My concern in this chapter is only with what a right not to work reveals about the egalitarian implications of the strain of liberal theory that Rawls's work launched.

After some clarifying remarks on idleness, rights, and other notions relevant to the ensuing discussion, I will focus on *neutrality* and its role in liberal egalitarian understandings of justice. Then I will propose an argument supporting a right not to work that appeals both to neutrality and to the special characteristics of idleness or leisure. I will next reconstruct and comment on a well-known criticism of Rawls's treatment of leisure that corroborates my claim that liberal defenders of neutrality ought to support a right not to work. This argument, unlike the one that precedes it, does not depend on treating leisure differently from other consumption goods. Finally, I will address what I believe to be the principal source of opposition to a right not to work: the idea that such a right implies objectionable free riding. I will endeavor to diagnose the force of this contention and also to diminish its effect. Free riding *is* objectionable in almost all circumstances and considerations of fair play or reciprocity do militate against a right not to work. I will argue, however, that the demands of reciprocity are defeasible and that the case in favor of a right not to work can withstand challenges from this quarter—at least in the generally affluent societies of the "developed" world.

One way to implement a right not to work would be to provide state subsidies to idlers. But a more sensible way, from a public policy point of view, would be to provide basic income grants to *all* citizens unconditionally, a scheme advocated by Philippe Van Parijs among others.[1] By definition, a state that dispensed income *unconditionally* would not require beneficiaries to contribute in any way to the monetized economy. Irrespective of the economic and social merits of such a plan, would it be just? The case I will make for a right not to work implies an affirmative answer. However, I shall not have much to say here about unconditional income grants or, indeed, about institutional arrangements generally. My aim is only to show that Rawlsian liberalism can be brought to bear in support of the idea that a right not to work is just, and then to investigate some of the implications of this unanticipated conclusion for egalitarian theory.

Preliminary Clarifications

It is sometimes useful to distinguish "idleness" from "leisure" or from "not working" at a job. But for the present purpose I shall use these terms interchangeably. It is relevant that those who choose not to be employed almost always "work" according to some legitimate understandings of the term. To be

---

[1] See Van Parijs 1991, 1992a, 1992b; also Walter 1989; Webb 1990.

an "idler" is not necessarily to squander one's time in unconstructive pursuits. What individuals do when they are not working is relevant for the overall assessment of their idleness. But this issue should not be confused with questions about the relative merits of passing the time that is standardly allotted to paid employment in or out of the workforce. The objective here is not to judge the value of different types of activities, but to consider the justice of public expenditures for relieving material deprivations suffered by those who choose not to take paid employment.

One could defend policy positions that approximate those that would follow from an acknowledgment of a right not to work by distinguishing remunerative employment from productive contribution, and then arguing that only refusals to contribute productively to societal well-being should count as disqualifications for public provision. To be sure, the class of individuals remuneratively employed overlaps extensively with the class of productive contributors. But unless productive contribution is defined in market terms, these classes are not coextensive. Thus some people are paid handsomely for "work" that only doctrinaire free marketeers could construe as constructive, and others—homemakers, for example—contribute importantly to societal well-being without participating directly in the monetized economy. As remarked, many if not all voluntarily unemployed and underemployed individuals engage in socially constructive activities some of the time. It could therefore be held that hardly anyone is disqualified from public assistance altogether, even according to the intuition that underlies the conviction that the idle cannot legitimately demand aid. But since my aim is to engage recent liberal theory, I will not press this easier but less instructive line of argument. I will suppose instead that if there is a salary or wage attached to an activity or if it is done for profit, it is work, otherwise not. Needless to say, an individual can work and still lose money, especially if self-employed. For the present purpose, work is work in virtue of being done for remuneration, not because it actually is remunerative. It is this understanding that is assumed by adherents of the view that able-bodied adults ought not to live off the labor of others.

A right not to work implies public provision at a subsistence level or greater, such as would allow individuals to remain idle irrespective of their contributions to the monetized economy. We should be careful, however, not to let the idea of subsistence deflect attention away from considerations of justice. Despite the rightward drift of the prevailing political climate, most people today still believe that there ought to be a "safety net" for at least some of those, the "worthy poor," who are unable to survive by their own devices. Safety net measures can be defended by appeal to a duty to relieve suffering or to prevent individuals' lives from falling beneath a minimally acceptable level (see Goodin 1988). No doubt, one could defend the right of the voluntarily idle to subsist at public expense on these grounds too. It would only be necessary to show that voluntary idleness does not release the rest of us from the obligation to prevent individuals from falling below a certain level. Again, if my aim were only to defend the right of all people, including the voluntarily idle, to subsistence, this approach would be more direct and less controversial than the case I will go on to develop. But since I do not want to preclude implementations of a right not to work that involve provisions beyond what is necessary for subsistence, and since I want to use this more robust understanding of the right in question to investigate Rawlsian liberalism, I shall not press this line of argument either.

A right not to work implies "correlative obligations" on the part of others to do—or forbear from doing—certain things. The relevant other in this instance, now and for the foreseeable future, can only be the state. In practice, therefore, a right not to work implies a duty on the part of states to provide material assistance to the voluntarily unemployed. Thus the right in question is not simply a liberty that states are obliged to protect. The idea that the idle should not be coerced into the paid economy is uncontroversial. No one proposes to proscribe the idleness of the independently wealthy or of spouses of the well-off or indeed of anyone who does not ask the rest of us for support. The idleness of the poor is often viewed differently, especially in ungenerous times. Thus proposals abound nowadays to force the idle poor off public support and into the paid workforce, even as paying jobs diminish in number. But the popularity of proposals to force recipients of poor relief to work almost certainly has more to do with class and racial hostilities than with views about what fairness requires. It is worth noting too that so-called "workfare" is usually defended on paternalistic grounds, not by appeal to justice. The official aim is to counter a "culture of poverty" by breaking down habits of "welfare dependence." Even so, no one proposes to conscript the poor into the workforce. For one thing, labor conscription would be incompatible with the pro-market ideology that typically motivates attacks on welfare state provision. Worse still, labor conscription would offend against individual autonomy. In exceptional circumstances—in time of war, for example—it is arguably legitimate to force individuals to do what they will not undertake to do voluntarily, if coercing them is indispensable for some important public purpose. If we look to the recent past, however, it is fair to conclude that labor conscription is an expedient to which liberal states need never resort. To get people into the paid economy, market incentives almost always suffice. Conscription may be indispensable for raising armies, but not for mobilizing workers to produce the arms and matériel armies use.

In short, despite the fact that almost everyone believes that able-bodied men and women ought to add to the wealth of the societies in which they live, hardly anyone holds that states can legitimately force them to do so. Individual liberty takes precedence over convictions about how citizens should behave. It may also be that hostility toward free riding is muted or even extinguished in these cases because people believe that voluntary idlers who are not supported at public expense pay their own way, and therefore do not take unfair advantage of anyone else. In any event, a right not to work, construed as a liberty only, is relatively unproblematic. The problem arises only when it is proposed that states ought to make abstinence from paid employment materially feasible.

I note, finally, that the term "right" in the expression "a right not to work" accords with the understanding of most contractarian and utilitarian political philosophers, but not with that of John Locke (1690) or his intellectual descendants among contemporary libertarians. The word is intended to indicate a public policy position, very generally and at a high level of abstraction from actual institutional arrangements, that follows from more fundamental normative considerations. A right not to work, so conceived, is therefore not an infrangible constraint on public policy—to be violated only on pain of injustice. It is not, as neo-Lockeans would have it, a "premise" from which policy conclusions follow, but a "theorem" of the theory of justice in conjunction with pertinent empirical claims.

Neutrality

The idea that it would be unjust to provide idlers with public support is in tension with the conviction, emblematic of liberal theory after Rawls, that states ought to be neutral with respect to competing conceptions of the good. I will use "neutrality" to describe the way that liberal political institutions are supposed to work.[2] A neutral state neither favors nor impedes competing conceptions of the good—provided, of course, that they are compatible with the ideal of a well-ordered liberal regime. It would therefore follow that a liberal regime ought not to impede individuals from living in accord with conceptions of the good in which gainful employment is abhorrent or idleness esteemed, nor should it favor conceptions of the good in which participation in the monetized economy matters importantly. This is not to say that liberal states are under an obligation to insure that the idle and the industrious are equally successful in their various projects or, more generally, that all competing conceptions of the good fare equally well. What matters is intent, not outcome. What states are obliged to guarantee is that individuals' conceptions of the good coexist on fair terms.

I will oppose construals of neutrality that relieve the state of obligations to enable individuals to live in accord with their own conceptions of the good.

[2] My use of "neutrality" in this chapter therefore accords roughly with the account given by Ronald Dworkin (1978). It should be noted that Rawls himself has recently expressed reservations about this use of the term (Rawls 1993, 190–95). "Neutrality" is also invoked in recent liberal accounts of political legitimacy—for example, by Charles Larmore (1987) and implicitly also by Rawls (1993) himself. This rather different use of the idea will be discussed in Chapter 3. In that chapter, I will also show how the idea of neutrality joins the long-standing liberal commitment to tolerance with the moral philosophical conviction that equal respect for persons entails equal respect for their conceptions of the good.

But the case I will make for the justice of a right not to work does not follow from a general theory of an affirmative liberal state. The argument will depend instead on the nature of a right not to work, in the context of certain background assumptions about the world in which we live.

Strictly speaking, neutrality-based arguments for a right not to work underwrite public support for the voluntarily idle only in those cases in which idleness is motivated by a conception of the good. There could be no neutrality-based case for state support for weak-willed idlers, who believe they ought to work but are idle nevertheless, or for individuals who are idle because they are lazy. In practice, however, it is impossible to identify idlers' motivations reliably, and even attempting to do so would almost certainly involve unacceptably illiberal intrusions into individuals' lives. Thus there is no feasible way for those who would defend a right not to work on these grounds to distinguish worthy idlers from unworthy ones. If they conclude that the state ought to provide the former with support, they would be obliged to conclude that it must support the rest as well.

We must take care not to dissolve away the conflict between neutrality and the conviction that the voluntarily idle have no right to public support by construing neutrality in a way that recalls the classical liberal idea that individuals are free to do whatever is not forbidden by law, even when they are disabled by institutional arrangements from exercising their liberties. On that understanding, the requirements of neutrality would be met by any state that abstained from interfering with individuals' decisions about work or leisure. To contemporary ears sensitized to the demands of equality, however, this construal of neutrality has a hollow ring. We are free to the extent that we are able to do the things we want to do, not just to the extent that laws do not stand in our way.[3] This is why a right not to work implies correlative obligations on the part of the state.

This conclusion assumes that idleness is not an appropriate candidate for regulation or proscription by public authorities. From an orthodox liberal perspective, it plainly is not. Thus according to a widely acknowledged doctrine famously articulated by John Stuart Mill in 1859, individuals' lives and behaviors may be regulated only insofar as they harm others (Mill 1956). But on any likely account of harm — even one broad enough to encompass harm to society at large, not just to identifiable individuals, and expansive enough to identify "harm" with "making others worse off" — voluntary unemployment meets Mill's test. Idlers do not harm society in general, since even comparatively underdeveloped economies are able to reproduce themselves and to expand overall productivity while deploying only a fraction of the labor resources at their disposal. Even if we allow that withdrawing labor inputs constitutes a harm by making

---

[3] I defend this contention in Levine 1988, 20–39.

others worse off, the harm is negligible; and negligible harms do not justify public intervention. To be sure, idlers may harm themselves. But, for liberals, harm to oneself is not a reason for public interference either. There remains the question of harm to dependents. This is a gray area, partly in consequence of the way that traditional liberalism characteristically ignores questions about justice *within* households or family units. I would only note that there is no distinctively liberal reason to attribute responsibility to others in the way that received notions of family "dependence" assume. The dependents of voluntary idlers, if they suffer materially, suffer from a kind of bad luck. They therefore have claims of justice against the rest of us in the same way that others who suffer from bad luck do. It may be expedient to insist that individuals support their children and dependent spouses. Indeed, any of a host of reasons might weigh in favor of states enacting laws to this effect. But not considerations of justice. From that narrowly focused vantage point, possible harm to dependents would not justify proscribing or even regulating idleness.

It might be objected that arguments that weigh in favor of public support for the voluntarily idle prove too much, that they imply public obligations to subsidize all plans of life that can be held plausibly to follow from appropriate conceptions of the good. But since that level of public generosity would be absurd, defenders of liberal neutrality go wrong if they conclude that there is an obligation to subsidize the voluntarily idle. This objection is misleading, however. It obscures the respects in which plans of life requiring leisure can be relevantly unlike others, the vast majority, that the public is indeed under no obligation to support.

Is Leisure Special?

Consider individuals who, in accord with their conceptions of the good, would be idle were they not also needy. Do they have alternatives to paid employment? Without public or private provision, they can either work for a living, live on less than the minimal means of subsistence, or support themselves illegally. The last two possibilities are plainly unacceptable. Thus paid employment is the would-be idler's only genuine option. It is therefore fair to say that would-be idlers who work are effectively coerced into the labor market. They take jobs voluntarily, but only in the formal sense that liberals have come properly to eschew.

An obvious rejoinder is that liberals, committed to the idea that individuals ought to bear the costs and reap the benefits of their own free choices, have no cause to complain if leisure time, when it passes over into that part of the day ordinarily taken up by paid employment, is too expensive for most people to consume. Undeniably, the welfare of those who do not want to work is diminished by the high cost of leisure; their desires are less satisfied and they are less happy than they would be were leisure cheaper. Thus individuals with unusually strong preferences for leisure are worse off than they would be if leisure cost less. But the state's proper role cannot be to compensate for welfare deficits by satisfying expensive tastes. Seaside condominiums in posh resorts would also realize the desires and increase the happiness of many who cannot afford them. But the state is under no obligation to provide these luxuries. Neither therefore is it under any obligation to subsidize individuals who would rather be idle than work.

If this argument appears persuasive, it is because we are inclined to regard leisure as a consumption good among others, susceptible to being traded off for other things. Under the aegis of economic theory, it has indeed become commonplace to suppose that everything is at least to some degree substitutable. Why should leisure be different? Very often, it is not. In some, perhaps most, circumstances, there is no reason not to treat leisure like a fungible consumption good. But there are also cases in which this understanding offends the letter and spirit of liberal neutrality.

It is worth remarking that the commodification of leisure and even the distinction between work and leisure assumed throughout this discussion are to some degree specific to economic systems with labor markets, and that even today those engaged in "meaningful" or "creative" employment cannot always clearly demarcate work time from leisure.[4] From a less historically particular vantage point than the one economists and the philosophers who follow them suppose, work and leisure are not always distinguishable. But even when work and leisure are unproblematically distinct, as they are usually assumed to be, it is plain that, for some people, they coexist on a dimension of such importance to human life—and to conceptions of the good that give lives their coherence and identity—that they cannot be traded off against ordinary consumption goods except on pain of suffering a loss for which no compensation is possible. For some people, leisure is not an expensive taste at all, but a core constituent of a plan of life.

It is unlikely that there are people for whom leisure *for its own sake* is irreplaceable, people whose conceptions of the good center on leisure itself. It is difficult even to comprehend empathically how anyone could value leisure in this way. But there probably are a few people for whom leisure is irreplaceable in principle. These are people whose conceptions of the good lead them to undertake particular life projects that preclude them from taking paid employment, even when it available for doing just the things that they want to do. Thus it might be central to someone's life to be a *volunteer* teacher or nurse or charity worker in a way that is incompatible with being paid for doing these things and also with being otherwise employed. And there are surely people who, were they not effectively coerced into paying jobs, would be led by their conceptions of the good to pursue activities that, as a matter of fact, existing markets fail to reward—or to accommodate in sufficient numbers. Some of

[4] See, among others, Sahlins 1972; Gorz 1989; Block 1990; Schor 1991.

these activities have considerable nonmarket value, according to prevailing norms; some do not. Thus not only would-be child and elder care providers, poets, and artists but also surfers fall under this description. For all such persons, insofar as they are motivated by conceptions of the good, leisure is not an expensive taste but a core constituent of a plan of life, a fundamental value. In a word, it is special.

Similar considerations can be marshaled in defense of a right to paid employment.[5] To make the case that the state ought to accord such a right—by promoting full employment policies or serving as an employer of last resort—one would have to show that, for some individuals, the benefits of employment are such that nothing can adequately substitute for them. In this case too, it is unlikely but not impossible that a person would value job incumbency for its own sake. But there are many people who consider themselves able to pursue their life projects only by being gainfully employed. For them, work is special. It too is an irreplaceable component of a plan of life, not merely a taste.

For persons who consider their work special, what matters is not just the pecuniary benefits of paid employment, since direct grants can always substitute for wages. It is the fact of employment itself. That this could be so is, of course, a consequence of many historically contingent factors. Thus it is almost certainly relevant to any likely defense of a right to work that individuals generally cannot purchase jobs and that employers buy employees' services while employees do not buy employers. It is also relevant that social norms are such that participation in the monetized economy is, for most people, a basis for self-respect and the respect of others.

The claim that work is special depends on background considerations of this sort and on the intrinsic nature of work, but not on the underlying justificatory strategy that proponents of a right to work endorse. The nonsubstitutability of paid employment can be defended on utilitarian or perfectionist grounds by appeal to some notion of self-realization or in a variety of other ways. The point is just that for at least some individuals some of the time, nothing can compensate satisfactorily for the lack of a paying job. In the same way, it is not necessary to endorse a particular justificatory strategy to defend a right *not* to work. Leisure too can be an intrinsic, nonsubstitutable component of particular conceptions of the good, a fact that any plausible underlying moral philosophy can easily accommodate. Like employment in the monetized economy, idleness can sometimes be so connected to individuals' self-understandings, to their rela-

---

[5] Richard Arneson (1990), Jon Elster (1988), and J. Donald Moon (1988) argue against state provision of a right to work but in a way that supports the contention that work is special in the indicated sense. They each maintain that in existing circumstances employment of the involuntarily idle by the state cannot adequately realize the nonpecuniary benefits of paid labor. Elster argues, in addition, that implementation of a right to work by states would have detrimental macroeconomic effects.

tions with others, and indeed to their very identities that trading off leisure for a wage can only be to the detriment of what matters fundamentally from a normative point of view. This, in sum, is why leisure cannot always be treated as an expensive taste. To view it as one among *n* axes in an individual's consumption space is to deny that it is special.

It is possible, of course, that *anything* an individual might value could have comparable intrinsic importance in that individual's plan of life. But this is not in fact the case. In societies like our own, very little is special, at least to a degree that should concern policy makers committed to neutrality. What makes leisure—and also work—special is the role that paid employment plays in our form of life: for almost all of us, *being employed* matters.[6] The claim that an unusual preference for leisure ought not to be treated as an expensive taste is made true, as it were, by the way the world is.

In later chapters, I will defend the idea that the (social) world can be profoundly transformed, indeed that it can be changed in ways that dissociate contribution and distribution even more radically than would be the case in a world otherwise like our own that acknowledges a right not to work. In a world like the one I will sketch, current understandings of work and leisure would, in all likelihood, change so profoundly that neither a right not to work nor a right to work *could* matter fundamentally to anyone's plan of life or conception of the good. In our world, however, work and leisure do matter; for most of us, they matter overwhelmingly. This is why both are *special,* and why neutral political institutions have to accord both their due.

Leisure in excess of the amount normally allotted to those who work a standard working day can sometimes be purchased in a way that paid employment generally cannot. But for anyone who depends on a job for income, leisure can be purchased only with money gained from paid employment, a prospect that defeats the idea of living in accord with a conception of the good for which idleness is mandatory or paid employment abhorrent.[7] In contrast, ordinary consumption goods are paradigmatically substitutable. Seaside condominiums can

---

[6] Academic readers who are skeptical of this claim might try the following thought experiment. Consider two states of the world: in one you have an academic appointment with no teaching or administrative duties and a level of compensation sufficient for your needs. In the other, you have the same level of compensation (from an inheritance, say) but no academic position and therefore, as in the former case, no duties. I would venture that nearly everyone would have a strong preference for the former situation And I think that the reason is not so much the honorific status that we assume would attach to an appointment without teaching or administrative duties but the fact that we would be employed in the one case but not the other. Paid employment or its absence matter in our culture—irrespective of the pay and even of the nature of the employment itself.

[7] However, individuals with nonwage income—beneficiaries of direct state provision, for example—are able to purchase employment indirectly in the sense that they are able to assume occupations that they might not otherwise be able to "afford."

figure in the realization of particular conceptions of the good. But they are not of such importance, even for individuals bent mainly on particular styles of consumption, that they cannot be replaced by other goods without the loss of what matters intrinsically. On the other hand, if leisure is for some individuals what work is for others, no substitutions are available. Of course, would-be idlers will usually accept paid employment "voluntarily" inasmuch as they need food, clothing and shelter that they are otherwise unable to obtain. But the income that accrues from work is not a substitute for leisure in the sense that a house in the mountains might substitute for a seaside condominium. To be compelled by circumstances to take employment, in opposition to one's own conception of the good, is to be unable to do what matters fundamentally to oneself. Individuals in this situation are effectively disabled from pursuing their distinctive plans of life. They are denied equal treatment by prevailing institutional arrangements.

Liberals are in no way committed to the idea that states are obligated to satisfy the expensive tastes of individuals whose desires exceed their budgetary constraints. But they are committed to according persons equal respect. To do so, they must insure that individuals have equal opportunities to obtain what matters fundamentally to them. Opportunities to obtain what matters fundamentally are means for pursuing projects that follow from conceptions of the good. Neutral states will treat such projects fairly. They will guarantee equal opportunities for pursuing whatever falls within the acceptable range of particular conceptions.

Just as states are not obligated to satisfy expensive tastes, neither are they under any obligation to insure that individuals succeed in their various pursuits, however important these pursuits may be to those individuals. A person who undertakes to become, say, a concert pianist cannot claim a right to be provided with concert halls and audiences. However, a neutral state will effectively accord this individual a right to the means for cultivating the talents that warrant playing before audiences in concert halls—that is, for pursuing the project of becoming a concert pianist under favorable conditions. Similar considerations obtain for those whose conceptions of the good are, for any reason, incompatible with paid employment. There is no obligation on the part of the public to insure that they succeed in their particular endeavors, whatever they might be. But states ought to allow them to pursue their objectives under conditions as favorable as those in which their fellow citizens, for whom leisure is not special, pursue their own various ends.

Idleness and the Difference Principle

What I have said, so far, about a right not to work has depended on a particular construal of neutrality and on the contention that leisure is special. There are, however, other resources within the liberal arsenal that support a right not to work that do not appeal to this contention. Even Rawls's account of justice (1971) can be enlisted in defense of this right, despite his express opinion to the contrary (Rawls 1988).

The main aim of *A Theory of Justice* is to develop principles to regulate the fair distribution of "primary goods" at the level of a society's "basic structure," its fundamental economic, social, and political institutions. Primary goods are resources instrumental for the realization of any of the particular conceptions of the good individuals are likely to hold. Rawls maintains that where genuine equality of opportunity obtains, primary goods other than basic rights and liberties, which he would have distributed equally and to the greatest extent possible, may be distributed unequally if and only if the resulting inequalities *work to the advantage of the least well off.* Rawls calls this requirement the Difference Principle.

The Difference Principle is intended to articulate the demands not of equality per se but of egalitarian justice. Thus, instead of mandating strictly equal shares, it asserts a presumption in favor of equal distributions of the relevant primary goods. If the presumption is overcome, unequal distributions are justified. But the burden of proof lies with whoever would propose unequal distributions, and what must be shown to meet that burden is that an unequal distribution can be expected to enhance the share of primary goods going to the least well off. Insofar as incentive structures that reward the exercise of talents and the expenditure of effort differentially can spur productivity in ways that benefit the least well off, strict equality and egalitarian justice can diverge. When they do, equality must give way. Nevertheless the Difference Principle expresses egalitarian concerns. It articulates the idea that egalitarians want the best possible equal treatment for all. Unlike equal treatment *tout court,* this end cannot be achieved by leveling down. It requires instead that we bring the bottom up.[8]

Rawls's account of justice bears importantly on the issue of a right not to work, though not, as remarked, in the way Rawls himself believes. We have seen how opponents of a right not to work appeal to deep and long-standing intuitions. Rawls endorsed these intuitions too, even to the point of revising the Difference Principle slightly to accommodate them—after it became clear that his original formulation of the Difference Principle conflicts with them. Rawls's emendation of the Difference Principle and the spirit behind it have been challenged by Van Parijs (1991), however. A brief overview of the Rawls-Van Parijs dispute will show that, *pace* Rawls, partisans of neutrality can defend

---

[8] As noted, the Difference Principle applies only after basic rights and liberties are distributed equally and to the greatest extent possible. If, as Rawls insists, basic rights and liberties are accorded their "fair value"—in other words, if the conditions necessary for their equal distribution (to the greatest extent possible) are in place—then, arguably, we are moved even more in the direction of strict equality than we are by the Difference Principle alone.

a right not to work on Rawlsian grounds, without appealing to the difference between leisure and ordinary consumption goods.

Van Parijs's case against Rawls revives a consideration central to Richard Musgrave's critique of *A Theory of Justice* nearly two decades ago. However, Rawls's current view—and the position assumed in Rawls's writings subsequent to Musgrave's critique—effectively incorporates Musgrave's criticism of his original account of the Difference Principle.[9] Musgrave showed that the Difference Principle, as formulated in *A Theory of Justice,* perversely favors individuals with higher than average preferences for leisure. This, for Musgrave, is a consequence to be deplored. It is not entirely clear why, but it is safe to assume that a large part of the explanation lies with Musgrave's conviction that it would be unjust to favor able-bodied idlers. In light of the way liberal theory has developed since the Rawls-Musgrave exchange, however, we might say that a better reason for taking exception to this result is that it betokens a violation of neutrality. A state that implemented a right not to work would effectively promote idleness over more industrious pursuits.

The way to avoid a redistributive system that favors individuals with higher than average preferences for leisure—holding talents (innate earnings abilities) constant—is, Musgrave argued, to equalize "goods and leisure potentials" (understood as "potential welfare") through lump-sum taxation.[10] But this proposal, because it assumes that welfare is the proper distibuand, is unavailable to Rawls. His principles of justice regulate the distribution of resources, primary goods, not welfare. Thus Rawls adopts a different strategy to achieve a similar end. In order not to favor the lazy over the industrious, Rawls modified the Difference Principle, adding leisure to the list of primary goods. He proposes that "twenty-four hours less a standard working day . . . be included in the index as leisure. Those who are unwilling to work would have a standard working day of extra leisure, and this extra leisure itself would be stipulated as equivalent to the index of primary goods of the least advantaged" (Rawls 1988, 257). In this way, Rawls "corrects" the bias Musgrave identified while retaining a primary goods metric.

It is fair to say that Rawls's aim in revising the Difference Principle, even at the outset, was to restore neutrality. As Van Parijs has pointed out, however, Rawls's revision introduces a contrary bias—against those who value leisure highly. To see why, suppose that we have a distribution D_I that satisfies the Difference Principle (corrected in the way Rawls suggests). Then suppose that an exogenous change is introduced that makes it possible to improve the share of

---

[9] See Musgrave 1974. For Rawls's (concessionary) reply, see Rawls 1974, 1988.

[10] Strictly speaking, Musgrave would "maximin," not equalize, goods and leisure potentials. That is, he would maximize the minimal share in just the way (and, presumably, for just the reasons) that Rawls would maximin individuals' shares of primary goods (excluding basic rights and liberties) generally.

primary goods going to the least well off—perhaps a new technology is developed or a reserve of natural resources is discovered. It is evident, Van Parijs concludes, that "the consistent implementation of Rawls's proposal requires that the (additional) funds . . . be used as a subsidy that is proportional to the number of hours worked" (Van Parijs 1991, 109–10). If the subsidy were more than proportional, the primary goods index of full-time workers would grow faster than that of part-time workers; if it were less than proportional, the index of part-time workers would grow faster than that of full-time workers. The resulting distribution D_2 would therefore be like D_1 except that everyone would have additional resources in proportion to how much they worked. This result does accommodate the deeply entrenched intuition about idleness that led Rawls to revise the Difference Principle. But it plainly violates neutrality. It introduces a bias favoring some conceptions of the good over others.

Of course, even to implement Rawls's proposal, it would be necessary to develop a theoretically well motivated way to determine what counts as work and leisure, and to develop a work and leisure metric. These are serious problems, perhaps insoluble ones, given the essential historicity of the concepts involved. Proponents of Rawls's idea would also need to address a difficulty long held to afflict schemes to distribute benefits in proportion to productive contributions. The problem is that on standard neoclassical assumptions, making one's distributive share depend on one's productive contribution conflicts with efficiency (Pareto optimality) because it provides excessive incentives to work. Under D_2 wages would be higher and therefore leisure would be more expensive. Then those who prefer leisure to increased shares of consumer goods would be worse off, and the result would be Pareto suboptimal because individuals with strong preferences for leisure would have to work more than they do in D_1 in order to maintain their welfare positions. This worry is, to some extent, an artifact of the identification of efficiency with Pareto optimality, in other words with a notion that is useful for purposes of economic analysis but is nevertheless at some remove from intuitive understandings of what efficiency involves. Nevertheless, even left-wing economists have found this consideration compelling. Van Parijs notes, for example, that it was in order to maintain efficiency wages that Oscar Lange (1936–37), in his seminal discussion of market socialism, abandoned the idea that the "social dividend" on publicly owned capital be distributed as a function of competitive wages. Lange concluded that, for efficiency's sake, the social dividend ought to be distributed equally among citizens irrespective of their contribution toward its production.

Pareto optimality is a welfarist criterion; therefore Rawlsians and other resourcists, insofar as they are concerned with justice (and not also efficiency), need not be alarmed. There is, however, a similar objection that does embarrass Rawls's stipulation that a standard working day of extra leisure ought to be counted as the equivalent of the index of the primary goods of the least advantaged. To put it briefly, in Rawls's proposal the value of the primary goods held

by the voluntarily unemployed would rise *fictionally* with an exogenously in-
duced increase in the share of primary goods going to the least well off. Since,
according to Rawls's stipulation, the cost of leisure would rise, the holdings of
the voluntarily unemployed would be deemed larger, although in fact they
would have the same resources than they formerly did. This result is untenable,
just as its welfarist equivalent was. So, therefore, is the stipulation that accounts
for it. In a word, Van Parijs is right: Rawls's revision of the Difference Principle
introduces just the opposite bias from the one Musgrave identified. It favors
those whose conceptions of the good lead them to work more. As remarked,
this bias accords with long-standing and widely held intuitions that Rawls
shares. Perhaps it could be defended on perfectionist or utilitarian grounds,
that is, by recourse to justificatory strategies of the kind that Rawls expressly
avoids. But it is unjustifiable insofar as the point is to treat individuals' conceptions of the good fairly. To be fair to idleness, the state would have to acknowledge and enforce a right not to work.[11]

A Free Rider Problem?

I would venture that the broad consensus against public support for the voluntarily idle rests, in large part, on the idea that it is wrong to reap benefits
without paying the costs incurred in their production. Publicly supported idlers
would be free riders, and free riding is, on the face of it, objectionable. But it is
a mistake to deduce opposition to a right not to work from a generalized opposition to free riding as such. Contrary to what is widely (if unreflectively) assumed, free riding is frequently unavoidable and not always indefensible. Even
so, the kind of free riding that a right not to work implies might nevertheless
always be objectionable or, more plausibly, objectionable in the context of relevant background conditions. If so, a right not to work ought not to be provided, notwithstanding the demands of neutrality or the implications of Rawlsian justice. But this is not the case. Legitimate concerns about free riding do
not successfully undermine these distinctively liberal arguments for a right not
to work.

We should take care not to confound worries about the effects of free riding
in collective action problems with questions about the normative status of free
riding. Free riding problems typically arise in connection with the production
of so-called public goods, goods that are jointly produced and/or effectively
nonexcludable.[12] It is widely assumed that public goods would be underpro-

---

[11] Van Parijs (1991) goes on to maintain that resource egalitarianism permits a move from D_1 to
D_2 without favoring either the lazy or the industrious.

[12] Public goods have been variously construed in the literature. Garett Cullity (1995, 3–4) lists a
number of other properties sometimes ascribed to public goods.

duced or not produced at all in instances in which individuals would prefer free riding to contributing toward their production. The prospects for public goods provision are particularly dire in those very common situations that are modeled by the so-called Prisoners' Dilemma: where, in addition to preferring free riding to cooperation, individuals prefer least of all that other individuals free ride on their own productive contributions.[13] But since it has been assumed throughout this discussion that a right not to work would be implemented by states, this worry is of no consequence here. As Hobbes (1651) made clear long ago, states are always able to "solve" collective action problems by compelling compliance through the use or threat of force. In any case, my concern is with the justice of public support for those who choose not to work, not with difficulties in the way of implementing the provision of such a right.

There is a widespread belief, articulated by Herbert Hart (1955), according to which accepting a benefit creates a liability to contribute to its cost of (re)production.[14] Those who fail to execute these obligations act wrongly because they violate a norm of reciprocity or fair play. By receiving without giving back—or giving back enough—they take unfair advantage of others. If free riding is understood as taking unfair advantage, and if the point of a theory of justice is to elaborate what fairness requires, then free riding would of course be unjust, and the injustice of voluntary idleness would follow directly. But this conclusion is too hasty. I will not challenge the idea that voluntary idlers are free riders, nor the contention that, as such, they take advantage of others; nor will I deny that, in doing so, they offend against fairness. What I will question is the conclusion that the kind of unfair advantage that publicly supported idlers take is, on balance, objectionable. Because voluntary idlers do free ride, there is indeed a sense in which a charge of injustice that can be leveled against a right not to work. But this reproach is swamped by countervailing considerations—including considerations internal to the idea of justice itself.

Perhaps the most direct way to see that the case for a right not to work can withstand the free rider objection is to realize that the principle on which this objection rests would tarnish nearly all social interactions. The problem is not only that, for a wide range of human interactions, there is no uncontroversial way—and sometimes even no conceivable way—to determine real costs and

---

[13] In a Prisoners' Dilemma, each individual prefers most of all to "defect" when others "cooperate," then to cooperate when others cooperate, then to defect when others defect, and least of all, to cooperate when others defect. Then if all players choose what is individually best, they will each defect, and the public good will not be produced. For a comprehensive account of game theoretic reconstructions of collective action problems, see Taylor 1987.

[14] Hart's principle of fairness or fair play is anticipated in Broad 1916. A similar thought is articulated in Rawls 1971, 111–12. See also Simmons 1979, 101–42. Hart proposed this principle in an effort to account for political obligation. There is no reason, however, not to extend its applicability to cooperative schemes generally.

benefits.[15] The deeper problem is that even if we could agree on what it means to "get what we have paid for," hardly anyone would ever get precisely (or even approximately) that much; for there is generally no way to coordinate individuals' behaviors that is not significantly redistributive. Whenever the "payoffs" from individuals' actions depend, in part, on what other individuals do, some persons will give more than they get, while others will get more than they give.

Thus there are few, if any, public goods whose benefits do not affect individuals differentially—in ways that fail to correspond proportionally to individuals' contributions toward the production of these goods. Almost without exception, therefore, whenever a public good is supplied, some individuals are in varying degrees free riding on the contributions of others. And even if we could somehow get the accounting right among ourselves, it would remain the case that each of us always free rides, as it were, on the culture, knowledge, and techniques that are every living human being's inheritance from preceding generations. Thus we are bound sometimes to play the sucker and sometimes to benefit from the fact that others will be suckers for us (see de Jasay 1989). Free riding and being free ridden upon are inexorable facts of our existence as social beings. Unless we are prepared to condemn what is impossible to avoid, there can be no general proscription of free riding. Opposition to a right not to work cannot therefore be deduced from the ostensible reprehensibility of free riding as such.

Still, there is a prima facie case against free riding, and voluntary idlers are not exempt from its scope. Can opponents of a right not to work maintain that this prima facie case remains in force after all relevant factors are taken into account? I have argued that liberals who have taken the Rawlsian turn ought to answer no. However, it is worth reflecting on why this conclusion remains counterintuitive. My suggestion is that the lingering effect of a way of thinking that was once reasonable but that is rapidly becoming obsolete provides a large part of the explanation.

There can be little doubt that the virulent, material scarcities that have afflicted humankind throughout its history have profoundly conditioned intuitions about fairness that persist to this day. The long-standing hostility to voluntary unemployment is an understandable functional adaptation to this apparently inexorable fact of human life. But acute scarcity has subsided with the expansion of productive capacities under the revolutionizing aegis of modern capitalism. Why, then, has this conviction survived virtually intact? The maldistribution of already existing affluence is certainly part of the explanation;

---

[15] Market transactions are the one clear exception, but only insofar as conditions obtain such that market prices represent or at least approximate efficiency prices. In any case, where reciprocity is at issue there are seldom posted prices at all. Typically, there are only unreliable shared understandings and vague intuitions.

because of it, significant scarcities persist almost everywhere. I would submit that in societies that are generally affluent, the scarcities that make voluntary idleness continue to seem unconscionable owe more to social inequalities—indeed, to palpable injustices—than to any material inability to achieve levels of affluence sufficient to support a generalized tolerance of free riding. My claim, in other words, is that the conviction that militates against a right not to work is a residue of a historical moment that, no longer obtains, at least in the "developed" world.[16]

As remarked, one could argue that most, if not all, principled idlers do in fact contribute constructively to the well-being of working members of society—that they do *something*, even if they are not paid for it. Perhaps one could even argue, on this basis, that voluntary idlers meet the requirements of reciprocity after all, and therefore that they are not really free riders. But as I declared at the outset, there is no need for a liberal to appeal to an understanding of productive contribution *outside* the paid economy to defend a right not to work. Liberals can concede that voluntary idlers free ride. They can concede too that their free riding is objectionable. But the fact that voluntary idlers free ride is not a consideration of sufficient weight to counter the case for a right not to work. Their free riding is of insufficient weight for just the reason that it is no longer a reasonable functional adaptation to real-world conditions to demand that everyone do their "fair share" in the face of scarcity. Increasing affluence diminishes, without extinguishing, the moral urgency of reciprocity. At the same time, it enhances the importance of doing what is required to implement values that may conflict with reciprocity—neutrality among them. In general, reciprocity and neutrality work in harmony. But in affluent societies they conflict when the issue is a right not to work. Then, I maintain, reciprocity, should give way. The reason is plain. The more scarcity there is, the more pertinent reciprocity is. With increasing affluence, its urgency recedes.

It has long been recognized that justice and therefore the kind of injustice that free riding exemplifies matter less as the circumstances of justice—above all, scarcity itself—diminish in importance.[17] With decreasing scarcity, intuitions formed when free riding mattered more lose their force, even as they linger on. But the idea that basic societal institutions ought to treat persons equally remains intact. Neutrality therefore comes into its own, effectively swamping the free rider concerns raised by a right not to work.

---

[16] In pressing this point, I am of course assuming that however much justice may require the *redistribution* of wealth from affluent countries to poor ones, well-off countries are not obliged to transfer so much wealth that they would no longer be sufficiently affluent to sustain genuinely liberal political regimes.

[17] On "the circumstances of justice," the conditions under which justice matters, see Chapters 2 and 5 below.

Whether of not we are now at a point where reciprocity ought to be of scant concern is, of course, debatable. I have already registered the opinion that we are potentially at that stage now, and would be there in fact if only existing wealth were more equally distributed, but I will not press the point here. Nor shall I venture an opinion on whether, taking all relevant factors into account, the world or (more likely) some part of it ought actually to accord a right not to work. My claim is only that recent liberal theory contains resources that support the provision of such a right, at least in affluent societies, and that intuitions that suggest contrary positions are largely residues of historically superseded real world conditions. *Pace* Rawls, but from a generally Rawlsian point of view, a right not to work is not blocked by considerations of justice. Fairness to goodness implies fairness to idleness too.

Thus liberal egalitarianism dissociates contribution from distribution to a remarkable and largely unacknowledged extent. But there is one connection that liberal egalitarians resolutely refuse to sever. They are determined to hold individuals responsible for the distributional consequences of what they freely choose to do. In Chapter 2, I will investigate this defining commitment—with a view, eventually, to putting it into question. To that end, it will be instructive to keep in mind how tensions *within* liberal theory resolve themselves when a right not to work is at issue. Rawlsian liberalism's capacity to tolerate free riding for the sake of its own distinctive theoretical commitments anticipates the way democratic egalitarianism can accommodate the indemnification of individuals even for the consequences of their own free choices—for the sake of deeper implications of equality itself.

2

What Do Egalitarians Want?

Egalitarians want equality. But equality as such, across all dimensions, is an impossible ideal. If individuals are equal in some respect—in resources, for example—then they are bound to be unequal in other respects—for example, in welfare—insofar as they transform resources into welfare differently, as they inevitably will. Egalitarians must therefore specify *what* they want to distribute equally. They must also justify why they accord one distribuand (or perhaps several) preeminence. This is what the "equality of what" debate is about.[1]

I begin by surveying some of the principal contending views in that literature as it developed in the 1980s and subsequently. Then I identify what is *liberal* about the positions in contention. The contenders are all generally Rawlsian in spirit, and I suggest that the aptness of the designation "liberal" has more to do with the comprehensive nature of Rawlsian liberalism than with more general features of liberal political philosophy—its emphasis on liberty, for example. I then introduce a topic that liberal egalitarians unwisely but characteristically ignore: the role of property, both private and public (or social), in the egalitarian project. That discussion motivates a resumption of the reflections on scarcity and affluence initiated in Chapter 1. It emerges that what egalitarians want—or ought to want—depends, in part, on levels of social and economic development. This consideration, along with others that I adduce in subsequent chapters, plays no role in the "equality of what" literature as it has so far unfolded. But it

---

[1] See Introduction, note 14.

is crucial to the critical evaluation of liberal egalitarianism and therefore also for ascertaining what a commitment to equality ultimately entails.

The Contenders

The "equality of what" literature can assume an arcane, even scholastic, character. But to grasp what is central to it, it is not necessary to follow every twist and turn. Nor is it necessary to focus on all contending views. The very cursory account that follows calls attention only to some aspects of leading positions and mentions only some of the major players. For expository purposes, it is convenient at the outset to describe these positions in terms drawn from "equality of what" writers themselves. We find, however, that a broad overview of the debate, based on the principal distinctions made in the literature, is only approximately useful for representing actual views.

A natural position to assume in the "equality of what" debate is that the egalitarian distribuand is whatever matters intrinsically. Thanks in part to the continuing influence of economic theory on social philosophy, "equality of what" writers typically identify what matters intrinsically with "well-being." Well-being egalitarians need not maintain that only well-being is an end in itself. It is compatible with well-being egalitarianism that there exist states of affairs, aspects of character, or properties of human agency that matter intrinsically, but that "well-being," on any of its usual construals, fails to pick out. What well-being egalitarians do believe is that if anything besides well-being matters intrinsically, it either falls outside the purview of egalitarian concerns or else matters for egalitarians qua egalitarians only in virtue of its effects on well-being.

It is usually assumed that well-being is *welfare* on one or another of the standard interpretations of that idea. Thus what matters intrinsically is identified either with happiness or, more generally, with some (felicitous) conscious state or with preference satisfaction.[2] This understanding derives from utilitarianism and its extensions in welfare economics. In light of this genealogy and in accord with contemporary usage, I will designate this position "welfarist." Recently, non- or extra-welfarist construals of well-being have been proposed. Sen (1992), for example, identifies well-being with "functionings," and G. A. Cohen

---

[2] See Dworkin 1981a. These claims are not strictly parallel. Those who identify welfare with some conscious state hold that this conscious state is intrinsically valuable (and perhaps also that it alone is). This contention may be false, but it is intelligible and even plausible. On the other hand, those who identify welfare with preference satisfaction cannot plausibly (or perhaps even intelligibly) claim that mere preference satisfaction is intrinsically (let alone uniquely) valuable. On this difference, see Scanlon 1991.

(1989) with "advantages," where functionings and advantages involve considerations that extend beyond welfare on any of its usual interpretations.[3]

Well-being egalitarianism stands in contrast to resource egalitarianism, the
idea that the equal distribution of means for obtaining what matters intrinsically is what egalitarians want. Following Dworkin's lead (1981b), it has become
commonplace for "equality of what" writers to construe "resources" broadly. A
resource is any means for obtaining what matters intrinsically. Resources need
not be external things. Thus talents are resources.

Another difference, orthogonal to the first, is between those who would
equally distribute some distribuand (or distribuands) directly and those who
would equally distribute *opportunities* for obtaining this (or these) distribuand(s).
These cross-cutting divisions, represented in the accompanying table, provide an
initial purchase on some of the more important positions taken in the "equality
of what" debate.

	Well-being	Resources
Outcomes	1	2
Opportunities	3	4

Welfare equality falls in box 1 and resource equality in box 2, though Dworkin's
account of it construes resources so expansively that it is reasonable to maintain
that it be placed in box 4.[4] Equal opportunity for welfare, Richard Arneson's
(1989) candidate, plainly falls in box 3. G. A. Cohen's (1989) contender, equal
access to advantage, straddles boxes 3 and 4, inasmuch as "advantage," an admittedly obscure idea, involves welfare (and therefore well-being) but also resources (at least in Dworkin's sense). Sen's (1992) claim that "capabilities" be
the egalitarian distribuand, where capabilities are opportunities for functionings, might best be put in box 3. But functionings involve more than well-being
on any of the usual understandings of the term, including the non-welfarist

---

[3] Sen (1992, 39) writes, "Living may be seen as consisting of a set of interrelated 'functionings',
consisting of beings and doings. A person's achievement in this respect can be seen as the vector of
his or her functionings. The relevant functionings can vary from such elementary things as being
adequately nourished, being in good health, avoiding escapable morbidity and premature mortal-
ity, etc. to more complex achievements such as being happy, having self-respect, taking part in the
life of the community and so on." Cohen (1989, 907) writes that "advantage is understood to include, but to be wider than, welfare." Although he is deliberately vague about what else he would
include, it is clear that what he has in mind is (at least some) "beings and doings."

[4] Dworkin 1981b. Arneson (1989), for example, argues that Dworkin effectively builds opportunities into his understanding of resources, and then faults him for contrasting resource equality
with straight welfare equality rather than the more analogous position, equal opportunity for welfare (which Arneson favors).

construal Sen favors. Thus the distinctions drawn in the table, however useful they may be for sorting out possible views schematically, are not always on point when applied to positions actually assumed by "equality of what" writers.

Rawls's case (1971, 1982) is especially difficult to classify. Since *primary goods,* the distribuand of Rawlsian justice, are resources, they would probably best go in box 2. But this categorization is problematic. For one thing, Rawls's position is not strictly egalitarian; only some primary goods, basic rights and liberties, are to be distributed equally come what may; others are regulated by the Difference Principle.[5] To be sure, the Difference Principle is egalitarian in intent. It mandates a presumption in favor of strictly equal distributions, and it accords priority to the least well off in order to diminish inequalities without leveling down. Thus it articulates what Rawls aptly calls "a tendency towards equality." Even so, it is not, strictly, a resource egalitarian principle. The other problem with placing primary goods in box 2 is that by focusing on means for implementing particular conceptions of the good, Rawls is more concerned with opportunities than outcomes. Thus if Rawlsian justice fits anywhere in the table, box 4 might be the appropriate place.

A position that would seem, at first, plainly to fall in box 4, but that antedates the "equality of what" debate in its current form, is implicit in Bernard Williams's account (1962) of equal opportunity. In "The Idea of Equality," Williams argued that for equality of opportunity to be achieved, there must be compensation for all factors causally contributory to distributional outcomes that are not themselves consequences of free (autonomous) choice. This exigency, Williams maintained, entails "material equality," an idea he did not further analyze. Arguably, therefore, Williams's equality of opportunity is a species of resource equality and should go in box 2, not box 4. But since he did not investigate material equality with the degree of care characteristic of recent treatments, there is no point in pressing the matter. Williams's contribution to the "equality of what" literature lies elsewhere. It was he who made the question of moral personality central to recent philosophical reflections on equality. On his account, the idea of equality presupposes a "Kantian" conception of the person, one which excludes empirically distinguishing features that are not freely (autonomously) chosen. What is not so chosen is arbitrary from a moral point of view. Thus whoever would have distributions accord with this understanding of moral personality would, other things being equal, want to redistribute in order to correct for the effects of morally arbitrary factors. If, as Williams insists, we are equal as moral personalities, our holdings should be equal too—except insofar as we make them unequal in consequence of choices we freely make.

---

[5] Again, the Difference Principle holds that unequal distributions are justified if and only if the inequality is likely to enhance the share (of appropriate primary goods) going to representative members of the group that is least well off.

Rawls's position on redistribution is less extreme. Distributions that result from morally arbitrary factors but that nevertheless accord with the Difference Principle are not only allowed but required. But Rawlsian justice rests on the concept of the person Williams identified, and this idea resonates throughout the "equality of what" literature. All participants in that debate at least partly dissociate morally arbitrary factors, ones that affect what individuals do or are, from claims about what individuals' distributive shares ought to be. They all agree that luck in "the natural lottery" (to use Rawls's expression) does not generate entitlements to external resources. But it would be hard to overstate the role that the natural lottery plays in generating actual distributions. It distributes inheritances, talents, handicaps, social and class positions, generational positions, and even the level of development of the societies in which persons live. The idea that there is a prima facie egalitarian case for nullifying the consequences of these factors, along with the (plainly arbitrary) effects of blind luck, is an extremely radical claim.

At the same time, all "equality of what" writers want to respect differences in the size of holdings that result from free choices. In their view, egalitarianism *requires* that individuals have *unequal* shares in consequence of the choices they freely make. I would venture that this exigency partly explains why the move from straight equality (of the right distribuand) to the equal distribution of opportunities (for obtaining the right distribuand) is appealing to many liberals. Equalizing opportunities seems to reconcile egalitarian aims with the defining liberal requirement that individuals be held responsible for the distributional consequences of what they freely choose to do. But there are liberal egalitarians who are strict outcome egalitarians, and for them, too, unequal distributive shares (of the right distribuand) are required—if, but only if, they are consequences of choices individuals freely make.[6] Following Williams's lead, individuals are deemed responsible only for what they do as "pure" moral agents. There is therefore at least a prima facie case for rectifying inequalities with other causal histories. Thus liberal egalitarians, unlike egalitarians *sans phrase,* do not want everyone to have equivalent shares (of the right distribuand). Their view of individual responsibility countervails this desideratum. But inasmuch as contingent and morally arbitrary circumstances generate nearly all the inequalities in existing distributions, liberal egalitarianism has extremely egalitarian implications, gauged by pre-analytic understandings. Nevertheless, its recommendations are not quite what we might expect egalitarians to want.

[6] Precisely how individuals might be held responsible for what they freely choose to do is more difficult to conceptualize for some proposed distribuands (welfare equality, for example) than for others (like resource equality), a fact that (partly) explains why Dworkin and others find resource equality appealing. But the claim is perfectly general. A liberal egalitarian who thinks that what egalitarians want is equality of welfare should be prepared to countenance situations in which individuals are at different welfare levels, insofar as their differences are consequences exclusively of choices for which the individuals in question are rightly held responsible.

Notwithstanding the Kantianism that pervades the "equality of what" literature, the fact remains that it is real people, not pure moral agents, who make choices that have distributional consequences. Thus Williams's account of moral personality, taken at its word, is too extreme to capture egalitarian aspirations or to help in adjudicating between contending distribuands. Rival positions in the "equality of what" debate represent different views of individual responsibility for distributional outcomes, different claims about what warrants indemnification and what does not. These understandings, in turn, represent different views of moral agency—all of them motivated by the Kantian idea of pure moral personality. The "equality of what" debate is therefore about what different positions on free choice and individual responsibility imply. To say that liberal egalitarians hold individuals responsible for the distributional consequences of the choices they freely make amounts to a description of the "equality of what" literature at a level of abstraction that overlooks differences between contending positions. Thus my characterization of liberal egalitarianism's defining principle is not intended as an endorsement of any particular contending view.[7] My intent instead is to describe the aim of all the contenders. Their common objective is to develop a theory of individual responsibility based on a broadly Kantian view of moral agency, where the morally arbitrary contingencies of the natural lottery hold no sway, and where the idea of individual responsibility is grounded in the notion of free (autonomous) choice.

To focus on free choice is, of course, to broach metaphysical questions about free will. But in the "equality of what" debate, as in political philosophy generally, it is assumed that these problems can be set aside. This understanding will be honored here. I would only remark that questions about free will and the possibility of autonomous choice almost certainly bear on all contending views in the same way.

---

[7] Readers close to the "equality of what" literature should therefore not conclude that I side with Cohen (1989) against Dworkin (1981b, 1988) in their dispute over the normative bearing of free (i.e., voluntary) choices. For Cohen, the aim of liberal egalitarians is to eliminate "involuntary disadvantages." He concludes, accordingly, that individuals are responsible for their preferences to the extent that they are voluntarily shaped, and that otherwise compensation is in order. However, one might worry that voluntary choice is too slender a basis for grounding a defensible theory of individual responsibility. People make choices because they have preferences and dispositions that are theirs in consequence, among other things, of their upbringing and general life experiences, factors over which they usually have little (voluntary) control. Dworkin (1988) defends resource equality against its critics by appeal to considerations of this sort; and Thomas Scanlon (1986) articulates similar claims in a more general context. My characterization of liberal egalitarianism's defining characteristic is intended to encompass both sides in this dispute. At issue is the normative status of *voluntary* choice and, more generally, the implications of a broadly Kantian understanding of moral agency for views of individual responsibility. What is not at issue is the idea that individuals are responsible for choices that are genuine expressions of moral agency or, what comes to the same thing, of their natures as free (autonomous) beings.

The "equality of what" debate engages issues in political philosophy, not metaphysics. But this literature has little direct bearing on practical policies or institutional arrangements. It is not, in the main, policy oriented, nor could it be. How, after all, could we expect to implement one position but not another, when we are obliged to rely on such clumsy means as state-organized redistribution of (monetized) resources collected through taxation? Thus, in practice, all egalitarian schemes underwrite measures to equalize income and wealth, and little, if anything, more. Indeed, it is far from clear what more an egalitarian *could* propose at a practical level. In short, the "equality of what" debate is about egalitarian ideals, not about egalitarian policy prescriptions. What is at stake is therefore of considerable moment for political philosophy. But the differences between positions taken within this debate imply little, if anything, about different courses of action egalitarians might actively pursue.

Liberal egalitarians would have persons bear the *distributional* costs and reap the *distributional* benefits of the choices they freely make. I will go on to question the urgency of this requirement, but I will not challenge the general impulse to hold individuals responsible for what they freely choose to do. As Kant (1959) long ago made clear, not to hold individuals responsible for their free choices is tantamount to not respecting them as moral agents. It is a plain violation of the categorical imperative. The supraliberal egalitarianism I will defend emphatically accords with this Kantian idea. What it challenges is not individual responsibility per se, but the pertinence of this idea to the distribution of benefits and burdens.

In any case, within a liberal egalitarian framework, where individual responsibility is "cashed out" in distributive holdings, a consensus view of what liberal egalitarianism's defining commitment entails remains elusive. Thus the "equality of what" literature has not yet reached a terminus. Perhaps it never will. Even so, this episode in recent social philosophy has succeeded admirably in establishing a distinctively liberal purchase on egalitarian aims and in revealing perspicuously what *liberal* egalitarianism is.

What Is Liberal about Liberal Egalitarianism?

It is, again, the conviction that individuals ought to be held responsible for the distributional consequences of their free choices that marks a position off as *liberal*. Historically, however, "liberal" has designated a position in political, not moral, philosophy. According to the received view, a political philosophy is liberal if it holds that there are activities and expressions of conscience that ought to be immune from state interference. Thus, from the inception of the liberal tradition in the seventeenth and eighteenth centuries, liberals have been proponents of limited government. Liberals today who endorse neutrality on the part of public institutions stand squarely in that tradition. But as their example attests, there is no principled reason why the designation "liberal" should apply only to governments. Indeed, by the mid-nineteenth century, the term was widely held to apply to a variety of social institutions, not just political ones. But it is only after the Rawlsian turn that "liberal" has been used to characterize a distributional principle. What, if anything, justifies this usage?

One answer might be that a position is liberal if it accords preeminence to liberty. There is merit to this contention. Liberty plainly is crucial to liberal political philosophy as it has developed historically and also to liberal egalitarianism. But this valuational commitment is by no means unique to liberalism. Thus the fact that liberty plays a central role in liberal egalitarian theory hardly warrants extending the traditional usage so drastically. I would propose instead that the reason why this term of political philosophy has come to seem apt in recent work on equality and distributive justice owes more to recent developments within liberal theory than to long-standing liberal convictions. It is, in other words, the Rawlsian turn—above all, the continuing influence of *A Theory of Justice*—that joins liberal and egalitarian concerns. This contention may seem paradoxical in light of the development of "political liberalism." But, as we shall see, Rawls's recent work is of a piece with his long-standing views about the nature of distributive justice. I develop this thought further in Chapter 3, but I have little more to say about liberal egalitarianism's "liberalness." In the end, liberalism is as liberalism does. It will be instructive, however, to elaborate briefly on the observation that support for liberty, though necessary, is hardly sufficient for designating a position liberal. Before pursuing liberal egalitarianism to its limits and beyond, it is well to recall that this quintessentially liberal value need not be articulated within the conceptual confines of liberal political philosophy, nor pursued by exclusively liberal means.

All liberals accord liberty pride of place. But many nonliberals do as well. Hobbes, for example, attached great value to liberty, which he defined as "the absence of External Impediments." Other things being equal, the more liberty the better. But other things are never equal. Given human nature and the human condition, unlimited liberty leads to a devastating "war of all against all"—to the detriment of people's fundamental interests, including their interest in liberty itself. Therefore individuals contrive a sovereign, "a common power to hold them in awe." The sovereign establishes order by forcing individuals to obey his commands. Sovereignty therefore restricts liberty; where the sovereign commands, the individual is unfree. But liberty remains a value. The sovereign governs best who governs least. Security must be assured, however, and security is impossible if freedom is unlimited. In "authorizing" a sovereign to act as their "representative," individuals terminate the state of nature, a condition of unrestricted liberty, thereby creating conditions in which, paradoxically, individuals' interests as free beings can be better served. Hobbes's case for sovereignty is therefore consistent with the interest in liberty that motivates liberalism. But Hobbes was no liberal. He inveighed against the very idea of limited sovereignty. In Hobbes's view, there is no aspect of individuals' lives or behaviors that the sovereign cannot rightfully infringe. A Hobbesian "minimal state" is therefore not the "minimal state" of classical liberal theory; it is not a state that acknowledges principled limitations to the use of public coercive force. But both the Hobbesian ideal of a sovereign who governs as little as possible and the minimal state of classical liberalism are motivated by a similar understanding of liberty and a similar view of its importance. Hobbes and the liberals are for liberty but at odds over the implications of this commitment. The fact that they can disagree in this way shows that support for liberty does not suffice to mark off a position as liberal.

Of course, it is not quite "the absence of External Impediments" but *autonomy*, self-direction or self-governance, that is served by holding individuals responsible for the distributional consequences of their free choices. Could this difference explain why "liberal," a term used originally to designate a view about the limits of state power, is now also used to describe a way of thinking about distributive justice? Some critics, liberal or otherwise, might think that it does, and go on to claim that this fact actually impugns liberal egalitarianism's standing as a "liberal" position. They might argue that traditional liberal political philosophers invoke one idea of freedom, the Hobbesian idea, while liberal egalitarians invoke another, autonomy, and that the use of "liberal" in both contexts only reflects a long-standing confusion that joins the two concepts into one. But this suggestion is a nonstarter: liberal egalitarians and traditional liberals do not invoke different concepts of freedom. In fact, a commitment to freedom in the Hobbesian sense implies support for autonomy in the sense assumed throughout the "equality of what" debate.

Perhaps the most perspicacious and influential effort to decouple liberty from autonomy can be found in Isaiah Berlin's essay "Two Concepts of Liberty" (1969). Berlin proposed to disaggregate extant understandings of freedom by differentiating autonomy and other forms of "positive liberty" from the "negative liberty" defended by Hobbes-in order, he maintained, to recover a genuinely liberal political theory committed only to freedom in Hobbes's sense. I will not address Berlin's subtle and frequently insightful arguments in detail here, but the outline of a rebuttal can be briefly indicated.[8]

A helpful way to describe the difference Berlin has in mind is through a metaphor he used himself: "negative liberty" designates an *area* within which individuals are unrestrained by others in the pursuit of their ends; "positive liberty" designates the *source* of control over an individual's behavior. Autonomy is therefore a species of positive liberty. Berlin's claim is that negative liberty, the

---

[8] I argue against Berlin's position in Levine 1981, chap. 10.

genuinely liberal ideal, is put at risk by positive liberty. At the extreme, a dedication to positive liberty underwrites a "totalitarian" politics dedicated to *rational self-determination* and therefore to determination of the less rational by the more rational—embodied institutionally in the State or the Party or even in a Leader. Positive liberty therefore threatens to usurp negative liberty altogether. Thus it is urgent, Berlin concluded, that positive liberty be excised from liberal theory.

It is far from clear, however, that a distinction between negative and positive liberty can be sustained at the level of abstraction Berlin assumes. Some years ago, Gerald MacCallum (1967) argued persuasively that freedom is a triadic relation joining agents, actions, and restraining conditions. Particular conceptions of freedom differ only in how the terms of this relation are construed. But at lower levels of abstraction, where conceptions of freedom generally do cluster around one or another of the governing metaphors Berlin identified, the considerations that make negative liberty an attractive ideal actually entail autonomy.[9] In brief, negative liberty is valuable not because the absence of constraints, External Impediments, is desirable in its own right, but for what it allows individuals to do. But being able to do what one wants, when one is not, as it were, the author of one's own ends, is as dubious a value as "the absence of External Impediments" itself. Thus it is reasonable to maintain that individuals are free when they do what they want, but only insofar as their ends are themselves freely chosen—in other words, to the extent that they act autonomously. If this is right, then, *pace* Berlin, support for autonomy ought to be—and generally is—as emblematic of liberal social philosophy as is support for negative liberty. Indeed, support for negative liberty implies support for autonomy too.

But although there is only one concept of freedom, there are different views of how that concept should be understood: views that interpret the terms in MacCallum's triadic relation differently or that emphasize negative or positive aspects of freedom. Even so, support for autonomy is still insufficient for designating a position liberal. Thus there are unabashed defenders of autonomy who are not liberals, just as there are defenders of "the absence of External Impediments" who are not. Marx is a case in point. By the early 1840s, Marx broke emphatically with the liberalism evident in his earliest writings. For better or worse, his subsequent view of political arrangements acknowledged no principled limitations on the use of public coercive force. But throughout his life Marx remained an ardent proponent of individual autonomy.[10]

[9] I elaborate on the argument that follows in Levine 1988, chap. 1.

[10] For further elaboration, see Levine 1993, especially chap. 6. I argue there that Marx's views, though certainly not liberal at the level of political theory, nevertheless imply support for liberal social and political institutional arrangements, at least under economic and social conditions conducive for moving from capitalism to socialism. These conditions include very high levels of economic development and a generally democratic political culture.

It is worth noting too that there are partisans of limited sovereignty—neo-Lockean libertarians, for example—who are not liberal egalitarians.[11] Libertarians regard state-organized redistributions of (idealized) market-generated distributions as infringements of infrangible property rights. They would therefore proscribe all but voluntary (and patently ineffective) redistributive measures undertaken for equality's sake—except for those that compensate victims of prior violations of property rights. In their view, individuals' holdings should be whatever capitalist markets determine, modified only by blind fortune and, of course, voluntary transfers. Thus libertarians' views differ markedly from those of liberal egalitarians. I will say no more about this strain of liberal theory here except to register the opinion that it rests on rights ascriptions that are patently arbitrary. For our purpose, the point is just that the existence of this form of liberal theory attests to the fact that liberal egalitarianism is not a position to which defenders of limited sovereignty need adhere.

Both traditional liberals and liberal egalitarians believe that liberty and autonomy matter fundamentally. Thus their positions reinforce one another. Arguably, they even suggest one another. But there is no stronger connection than this. At this level of generality, therefore, the most we can conclude is that there exists a certain affinity, perhaps only a family resemblance, between these species of self-proclaimed liberal theory. This impression will be reinforced when we turn to Rawlsian political philosophy in Chapter 3.

Private Property

Some little noticed assumptions in the "equality of what" debate call for scrutiny. Chief among these is the idea that what matters for egalitarians is the distribution of privately owned things. This assumption has two parts, one probably unavoidable, the other thoroughly contestable though seldom actually contested. What is almost certainly beyond serious dispute is that egalitarians ought to be concerned with the distribution of resources, even when their favored distribuand is non-resourcist. The reason is plain: there simply is no other feasible or (morally) acceptable way to distribute or (re)distribute any likely egalitarian distribuand. Thus even welfare egalitarians aim at an equal distribution of welfare through a particular resource distribution, a distribution that differs from straight resource equality because people differ in the ways they derive welfare from resources. Of course, welfare egalitarians could call for non-resourcist measures-state-sponsored harassment, say, or imprisonment or beatings-to bring the top down. But even were these methods morally permissible, as they surely are not, they would violate the egalitarian imperative to

[11] See, for example, Nozick 1974.

bring the bottom up. It is not clear that there are non-resourcist means, even morally impermissible ones, that could have that effect. I would therefore conjecture that we can dismiss non-resourcist routes to welfare equality. Similar considerations apply to equal *opportunity* for welfare. After legal and customary inequalities of status are dissolved and full political equality is achieved, there is no feasible way to distribute opportunities for welfare equally except through particular distributions (or redistributions) of resources. In the absence of any reason for thinking otherwise, it is fair to generalize this conclusion: the way to implement the equal distribution of any putative egalitarian distribuand, including all plausible non-resourcist candidates, is through one or another provision of resources to individuals.

On the other hand, it is not at all inevitable that resources be privately owned. Private ownership may seem unexceptionable. But it is well to recall that egalitarian impulses first asserted themselves within the socialist tradition, that is, within a political and intellectual current opposed to private property and committed instead to social ownership. Until recently, the idea of social ownership seemed unproblematic. The desirability of socialism was severely contested, of course, but no one doubted the cogency of the idea. Today this is no longer the case. Socialists tended unreflectively to identify social ownership with state ownership. It is now plain that state ownership is, at most, only one possible form of social ownership. The elaboration and defense of alternative forms of socialist property relations is a pressing question for socialist theory, perhaps the most pressing question today. But even allowing for the imprecision that we now know has afflicted the idea of socialism from its inception, a distinctively socialist purchase on the question "equality of what" is still viable. From a broadly socialist perspective, egalitarians should be less concerned with the distribution of rights to benefit from, utilize, and control assets privately, and more interested in the distribution of rights within cooperative enterprises and communities to benefit from, utilize, and control socially owned things.

The consequences of assuming private ownership are particularly salient in the case of resource equality. Resource egalitarians, on Dworkin's construal, would socialize the revenues resources generate (except insofar as they hold individuals accountable for the distributional outcomes of their free choices) but then distribute rights to utilize and control these resources privately. In this sense, their egalitarianism is partly, but only partly, "socialist."[12] They would socialize revenue rights but not control rights. Were revenue *and* control rights over most productive assets socialized, a very different perspective on what

---

[12] Resource egalitarianism resembles that strain of socialist theory that runs through the works of writers such as Tom Paine, Edward Bellamy, François Huet, César de Paepe and, above all, G. D. H. Cole. For these thinkers, the wealth generated by gifts of nature ought to be distributed equally and to everyone, but individuals should be able to retain the revenues generated by the productive contributions they themselves undertake. See Cole 1944 and Van Parijs 1991, 1995.

equality requires would suggest itself. Equality would then have to do with democracy or, more precisely, with the democratization of the economic sphere. I will elaborate on this idea in Chapter 5.

The "equality of what" literature has effectively taken over received understandings of the distinction between the state and the economy and their respective roles in allocating resources. Markets generate distributions; the state then redistributes the market-generated distribution, obtaining revenues through taxation and dispensing them through some combination of direct transfers and subsidies. The state also affects distributional outcomes through its fiscal and monetary policies and by providing public goods. Thus states are able to implement egalitarian distributions or, more precisely, to approximate them as best they can, given the clumsiness of the means at their disposal. In anything like the world as we know it, state institutions are indispensable for this task. Liberal egalitarians therefore look to the state to achieve equality. They accept market arrangements too, but with less enthusiasm. Unlike states, markets are not indispensable for organizing economic life. But with central planning in disrepute, there appears to be no *satisfactory* alternative to market mechanisms, no other way "to deliver the goods" at all well. Liberal egalitarians generally find little else to praise in markets, although their efficacy in identifying real economic costs is sometimes acknowledged, especially by resource egalitarians. Even so, liberal egalitarians do not argue, as "conservatives" do, that markets advance freedom or encourage desirable traits of character or sustain democracy. They rely upon markets *faute de mieux*, because they believe, as so many others do today, that alternative arrangements that would control economic processes directly are bound to be inefficient.

Because they would implement (or approximate) egalitarian objectives through state organized redistributions of the income and wealth that capitalist markets generate, liberal egalitarians are effectively, though not always explicitly, social democrats, in the sense that was commonplace in postwar European politics. But, as remarked, egalitarianism is in the main a creature of the socialist tradition. Unlike latter-day social democrats, socialists have long evinced hostility toward market arrangements—faulting them for the "anarchy" they introduce into economic life, for their role in undermining community, and, above all, for their inability to orient economic activities in ways that address fundamental human needs. Today these complaints seem either wrong-headed or irrelevant or both. Thus they fall on deaf ears, even among those who continue to identify with the socialist tradition. Hence the revival of interest in "market socialism," an idea that has been floated since the 1920s. Nevertheless, one reproach traditionally leveled by socialists against markets deserves notice here because of its particular relevance to the "equality of what" debate: markets, by their nature, remove the aspects of life they govern from democratic control.

In markets, individuals seek to make the best use they can of the resources they control, given the constraints they confront. Societal outcomes then emerge as unintended consequences of individuals' self-interested, maximizing choices. Thus societal-level allocations are never *directly* addressed. It is well known that this property of markets is helpful for dealing with the complex and interdependent information-processing problems that must be solved if economic assets are to be utilized efficiently. But this advantage is obtained at the expense of efforts to democratize the economic sphere. This consequence has important implications for the egalitarian project.

It is one thing for markets (partly) to regulate economic interactions and something else for them to generate the holdings that liberal egalitarians would have the state (partly) redistribute. It is clear, even in the absence of a sustained consideration of the role(s) markets might play in societies with socialized property relations, that any society that would count as socialist would have to eliminate or at least severely restrict markets in capital itself. Otherwise investment decisions and, more generally, control of society's fundamental productive resources would remain outside the domain of social control. It is also likely that in any socialist society wage rates too would have to be determined, at least in part, by nonmarket or extramarket considerations—if only because no constellation of forces capable of sustaining socialism politically could consign workers to their fate in unregulated labor markets. But with property socialized and labor markets constrained to some extent, the idea that markets distribute and states redistribute would no longer apply without qualification. The economy itself, the institutions that generate the distributions that the state redistributes, would be partly politicized. This fact has important implications for the defining liberal egalitarian conviction that individuals ought to be held responsible for the distributional consequences of what they freely choose to do.

Affluence

Many socialists, especially those who have taken Marx's theory of history to heart, believe that socialist property relations are appropriate only in societies with very high levels of material development. Socialism presupposes affluence. As we have seen in Chapter 1, affluence also bears importantly on the moral urgency of fairness and therefore, I would now suggest, on the "equality of what" question.

It has been recognized for many years that distributive justice matters to the extent that fairness is an urgent concern for those to whom benefits or burdens accrue. Thus the "circumstances of justice," the conditions under which the requirements of distributive justice are morally compelling, are now widely understood.[13] They involve both a "subjective" and an "objective" component. It

[13] On "circumstances of justice," see Hume 1896, bk. 3, pt. 2, sec. 2; Hume 1977, sec. 3, pt. 1; Hart 1961, 189–95; Lucas 1966, 1–10; Rawls 1971, 126–30.

will not be necessary here to dwell on the subjective component, the idea that individuals are generally self-interested. But to overcome liberal egalitarianism, it is crucial to reflect on scarcity, the objective side of the circumstances of justice.

Justice matters whenever cooperative interactions are both possible and necessary for generally self-interested individuals concerned to maximize their own distributive shares. In conditions of absolute scarcity, where cooperation will not expand the supply of goods to be distributed, awarding a benefit to one individual deprives another of it. Then there is no advantage in cooperation. Two individuals alone in a lifeboat with only enough water for one have nothing to gain from cooperation. If they are rational and self-interested, each will attempt to obtain all of the water. Were (nearly) everything absolutely scarce, the requirements of justice would be of no account. A society of this kind would be, as it were, beneath justice. On the other hand, a world of abundance would be beyond justice. Thus when air is abundant, as it normally is, there is also nothing to gain from cooperation. Relative scarcity stands between these extremes. A good is relatively scarce when not everyone can have all of it that they want, but where the amount accruing to individuals can rise if they cooperate in its acquisition. When the circumstances of justice obtain, most of the things people want are relatively scarce.[14]

So long as some goods, like being ranked first in an ordering, are "positional," such that it is logically impossible for everyone who wants them to have them; so long as others will, as a matter of fact, remain scarce no matter how developed productive capacities become; and so long as the many factors, including the inevitability of death, that force individuals to budget their use of time remain facts of the human condition, relative scarcity will be with us. But with the development of productive forces and an appropriate distribution of the economic surplus, relative scarcity can cease to structure and direct human life in the way that it has throughout human history. It can give way to affluence, though never, of course, to the kind of abundance that would make the distribution of benefits and burdens of no importance whatever. As relative scarcity is progressively (but never completely) overcome, the circumstances of justice diminish in saliency. In consequence, justice matters less or, what comes to the same thing, unfairness becomes increasingly tolerable.

Insofar as egalitarianism can be reduced to a substantive principle of justice, what holds for justice holds for equality too. Formally, justice requires that like

[14] Relative scarcity is not the only fact about the world that renders justice morally urgent. In addition, individuals must be sufficiently equal in natural endowments for cooperation to be mutually advantageous, and they must find themselves in circumstances where they are obliged to interact. Traditional contractarian accounts of "the state of nature" focus as well on these aspects of the human condition.

cases be treated alike: that instances be sorted out into morally relevant categories (or arrayed along a continuum determined by some morally relevant dimension) and that unequal treatment be accorded cases only if they fall into different categories (or stand in a different place along the appropriate continuum). Substantive principles of justice then provide content to the place-holder terms "like case" and "equal treatment" (see Perelman 1963). "To each according to merit," for example, is a substantive principle that would sort individuals into morally relevant categories according to how meritorious they are (or how meritorious their actions are) and would accord them unequal treatment in consequence. Or, on a finer grained understanding, individuals would be arrayed along a continuum according to their degree of merit (or the degree of merit of their actions) and compensated accordingly. In these terms, egalitarianism is the substantive principle "to each the same," where "each" designates all individuals (or some morally relevant subset of them). Egalitarians want this principle to govern the distribution of the egalitarian distribuand, whatever it turns out to be. Construing egalitarianism this way only restates the "equality of what" question. But restating it this way is instructive. It makes perspicuous the sense in which affluence diminishes the urgency of egalitarian demands.

Diminished urgency implies more than just mattering less. It alters the very nature of proposed distribuands, affecting what egalitarians want. The case of resource equality is illustrative. As remarked, the liberal egalitarian construal of the idea permits individuals to hold unequal resource shares. This result is plainly at odds with pre-analytic intuitions. But as relative scarcity is transformed into (near) abundance, the motivation for countenancing inequalities, even for (liberal) equality's sake, is reduced. In conditions of affluence, liberal egalitarians who believe in resource equality would therefore find themselves able to tolerate distributions closer to ordinary understandings. I will elaborate briefly on this thought.

It is plain that resource equality is not achieved, as we might naively suppose, when all individuals have equally constituted distributive shares. Thus Dworkin's account of resource equality (1981b) begins with a thought experiment in which readers are asked to imagine shipwrecked resource egalitarians arriving on a desert island where nothing is antecedently owned. They take it upon themselves to divide the island's resources equally. Since the items to be divided are not always physically divisible into equal shares, and since they are of unequal value to the individuals among whom they are to be distributed, Dworkin suggests that an appropriate method for bringing about an equal division would be, first, to find some currency (clamshells perhaps) that, for all practical purposes, is perfectly divisible, provide everyone with an equal amount, and then hold an auction supplemented by market exchanges. Assuming the competence and rationality of the shipwrecked immigrants, once the auction is completed and all markets clear, no one will prefer anyone else's commodity bundle to their own. What Dworkin calls the "envy test" will therefore be satisfied; no one's share of resources is better than anyone else's according to the judgments of the individuals themselves. Resource equality will therefore be achieved. But, of course, individuals' holdings will differ in their composition.

These differences can only multiply as time goes by and life on the island proceeds. Dworkin proposes a number of mechanisms, essentially hypothetical insurance markets, intended to maintain equality in the island's economy after the initial auction—in the face of production and trade and the vagaries of fortune. But he seeks to rectify only the differences caused by morally arbitrary factors. Because he is a liberal, Dworkin wants to hold individuals responsible for the distributional consequences of what they freely do with the resources they control. Thus the task is only to correct for the consequences of "brute luck." The term is Dworkin's, but I use it here not quite as he does, to designate "how risks fall out," but to describe all the consequences of factors that liberal egalitarians find morally arbitrary and therefore in need of rectification.[15] Dworkin contrasts brute luck with option luck, which he defines as "luck in gambles deliberately undertaken." If we understand "gambles" to designate outcomes of free (autonomous) choices undertaken in conditions of risk or uncertainty, then respect for the consequences of option luck is an important part of the liberal egalitarian theory of individual responsibility. In any case, the distinction is more analytical than practical. There will be few, if any, real-world cases that fall unequivocally in one or the other category. Consider, for example, individuals who contract diseases for which lifestyle factors are known to be implicated. To some extent, they are victims of bad brute luck. To some extent they gambled and lost.

Despite mechanisms in place for compensating for the (continuing) consequences of brute luck, individuals' holdings will come to differ in magnitude, not just in composition, as the initial auction recedes into the past. To see why, recall that preferences for leisure vary. With market arrangements in place, with or without public support for the voluntarily idle, individuals who value leisure highly will, as time goes by, have less to consume than individuals who lead more industrious lives. Those who expend less effort will therefore increasingly envy the commodity bundles of more industrious individuals. But, by hypothesis, they will not envy the leisure-commodity trade-off that these individuals have made. Dworkin therefore proposes that, for dynamic economies, we apply the envy test diachronically. Equality will be maintained if no one envies anyone else's distributive share (including their share of leisure) over the space of entire lifetimes. In this way, free choices will not disturb resource equality. But then,

---

[15] See Dworkin 1981b, 293. In Dworkin's usage, the distribution of talents is not a matter of brute luck in the way that, say, being struck by lightening is. But insofar as talents are innate, how talents are distributed *is* a matter of brute luck (according to the ordinary understanding of the expression)—in "the natural lottery." I shall therefore regard all causally relevant factors that affect distributional outcomes to be matters of brute luck, except insofar as the individuals to whom benefits and burdens accrue are properly held responsible for them. My usage therefore differs slightly from Dworkin's, but I think that it captures the idea he wants to express.

at all particular moments, individuals' holdings will differ—not just in their composition but also in their magnitude. In a resource egalitarian regime, in other words, there will be no time after the initial auction at which individuals' holdings will actually be equivalent. Dworkin's thought is that satisfaction of the diachronic envy test reconciles this result with the resource egalitarian's dedication to accord individuals equivalent resource shares. But it plainly does not, for even if individuals do recover a form of share equivalence when their lifetime allotments are taken into account, at any given moment individuals will not, in fact, hold equivalent shares. This outcome will come about not because *liberal* resource equality fails to obtain, but because it does.

This transparently counterintuitive result is incontrovertible from within a liberal egalitarian framework. With rising levels of affluence, however, it becomes increasingly feasible, normatively, to relax the principle that entails this conclusion. But if, as egalitarians, we are determined to go this route, then we must be prepared to nullify some of the consequences of option luck and of free choice generally. The idea that resource equality requires that everyone's holdings be the same is indeed an untenable dogma; equal shares need not be identical shares. But it is a liberal egalitarian deformation of the resource egalitarian ideal to maintain that equal shares need not be equivalent shares. The idea that motivates resource egalitarianism is captured in the auction Dworkin imagines in which shipwrecked immigrants acquire unowned things. But when Dworkin goes on to model features of dynamic market economies, resource egalitarian intuitions are effectively swamped by liberal egalitarian theoretical commitments. Because the lifetime is the time frame stipulated in the diachronic envy test and because lifetimes overlap, there can be no time in ongoing societies at which holdings actually are equivalent. Ironically, resource equality, as Dworkin conceives it, never actually obtains (after the initial auction), even when it is fully achieved.

To nullify the consequences of brute luck is to move in the direction of resource equality, as we understand the idea intuitively, apart from liberal egalitarian concerns. But to respect the consequences of option luck is to draw away from that ideal. However, as the circumstances of justice recede, equivalent holdings, or resource equality at all times, comes back on the agenda. In conditions of affluence, the way is clear to a concept of resource equality generous enough to accommodate the nullification of at least some of the consequences of option luck.

Paradoxically, however, this result will obtain only after distributional questions no longer matter very much. It is as Kafka said of the Messiah: "[he] will come only when he is no longer necessary . . . not on the last day, but on the very last" (Kafka 1946, 81). Why, then, insist on full resource equality? In a word, there is no reason to insist. As we will see in Chapter 5, by the time that distinctively liberal intuitions wither away (perhaps without ever disappearing altogether), egalitarian concerns will have developed to a point where they will no longer focus on the distribution of privately owned things. But for just this reason there will be less cause than there now is for anyone to resist strictly equal distributions of income, wealth, and other resources. The presumption favoring strictly equal distributions, equivalent shares, will have finally come into its own.

This conclusion carries over to any likely egalitarian distribuand proposed by "equality of what" writers. The more we approach abundance, the less urgent the demands of individual responsibility become. With ever increasing affluence, egalitarian aspirations take precedence over liberal impediments to full-fledged equality. Then differences that anyone who is not a liberal egalitarian philosopher would depict as inequalities can finally give way, and egalitarians can finally have what they want—or rather what they used to want—without *liberal* qualification.

Equality and/versus Fairness

It is because they identify with a generally Kantian view of pure moral personality that liberal egalitarians want to nullify the consequences of brute luck. This Kantian view also underwrites the liberal egalitarian conviction that it is wrong to indemnify individuals against some or all of the consequences of their free choices. Each position suggests the other, especially when relative scarcity makes fairness a morally urgent concern. Thus, intuitions that sustain the theoretical commitment defining liberal egalitarianism have entered into the common sense of our political culture. But deeply entrenched habits of mind are not logical implications, and egalitarians should be wary of what is widely assumed in a political culture that is less than fully cognizant, even today, of the implications of the level of affluence that already exists. Thus, as I claimed at the outset, a commitment to a generally Kantian view of individual responsibility does not entail that individuals be held responsible for the *distributional* consequences of what they freely choose to do. We are now in a position to see why.

The idea that there should be no indemnification for the distributional consequences of autonomous choices does not follow from support for autonomy per se. But it is necessitated by the impulse that underlies the deeply entrenched opposition to free riding discussed in Chapter 1, namely, the idea that the distribution of benefits and burdens ought to be fair. When a right not to work was at issue, fairness required reciprocity. But as we turn to the larger question engaged in the "equality of what" debate, fairness takes on a somewhat different aspect. Then fairness implies what liberal egalitarians maintain: that persons be held responsible for the chances they take and the efforts they expend. This view is implicit in the very idea of justifying distributive shares. When not everyone can have everything they want, everyone some of the time and nearly everyone all of the time will be unhappy with their share of one distribuand or another. But can aggrieved parties offer reasons for redress that others, if they are reasonable, would have to acknowledge? The answer will be yes, if and only if they are able to show that their holdings were unfairly allotted. The liberal egalitarian idea is that one can make such a case insofar as the natural lottery determines distributive outcomes, but that no one can reasonably expect others to heed their complaints about outcomes that result from choices the complainants themselves have made. When morally arbitrary factors are set aside, it is fair that persons reap what they sow.

The rationale for this cardinal tenet of liberal egalitarianism is implicit therefore in the burden of justification itself. As such, the liberal egalitarian's position is unexceptionable. What is problematic is its applicability in conditions of affluence. With increasing affluence, distributional outcomes stand in diminishing need of justification. When everyone has enough or more than enough, people care less about where they stand in the overall distributional pattern, and about the size of their own shares. They have less to complain about and less to justify to others. From a normative point of view, therefore, fairness matters less. If it is sometimes unfair to equalize shares of one or another distribuand, then so be it. As scarcity subsides, unfairness becomes increasingly tolerable, especially if there are more pressing, reasons—egalitarian reasons, for example—for breaching liberal egalitarianism's increasingly anachronistic defining principle.

The idea that, as scarcity subsides, unfairness becomes normatively more tolerable is similar to the conclusion I urged in Chapter 1. In this case, however, the problem is not that liberal egalitarians fail to appreciate how radical their own position is. The problem is with liberal egalitarianism itself. Liberal egalitarianism turns a consideration that is appropriate at levels of affluence that are very likely already (partially) surpassed into an infrangible matter of principle.

I will go on to argue that it is, ironically, for the sake of the values that motivate liberalism itself that even liberal egalitarians ought to acknowledge the limits of their dedication to holding individuals responsible for the distributional consequences of what they freely choose to do. To this end, it will be essential to embark on what may at first seem like a long digression. In Chapters 3 and 4, I turn away from egalitarianism per se to investigate some specifically political dimensions of liberal theory and practice. The case I have begun to make for an egalitarian theory *beyond* liberal egalitarianism is inextricably connected with the issues investigated in these chapters.

3

Political Liberalism

I use "political liberalism" to designate a way of thinking about political legitimacy that is closely allied with the "equality of what" literature. As I remarked in the Introduction, the term has come to be identified with John Rawls's recent work (Rawls 1993). Rawls's views are very much in contention throughout this chapter. But my use of "political liberalism" is broader than his. I use "political liberalism" to denote views about the nature and justification of political arrangements that center around the idea of *neutrality*, the notion I invoked (in Chapter 1) to defend a right not to work.

Political liberals, including Rawls, draw a line of demarcation between political and moral philosophy, insisting on the independence of the former from the latter. In doing so, they appear to dissociate liberal egalitarianism, a position in moral philosophy, from the liberal theory of the state, raising anew the question posed in Chapter 2: what is liberal about liberal egalitarianism? I have already suggested that the answer has mainly to do with the nature of Rawls's own political philosophy and the strain of liberal theory it has done so much to shape. By focusing on liberalism in general and political liberalism in particular, we gain a clearer perception of why this is so.

I begin by venturing some observations on liberalism generally, and then I consider connections between political liberalism and some traditional liberal positions. I argue that despite the evident merits of political liberalism and its connections with liberal egalitarianism, political liberalism is in no way superior to what I call "instrumental liberalism," a species of liberal theory that harkens back to the work of John Stuart Mill. I argue, however, that egalitarians have at least one good reason to prefer instrumental liberalism to its rival: it is more conducive to the eventual transcendence of liberalism's conceptual and political horizons.

The Received View

Traditionally, a political philosophy was deemed liberal if it acknowledged principled limitations on the use of public coercive force—in other words, if it held that the sovereign's authority over individuals' activities was subject to specifiable limitations. The kinds of interferences that liberalism proscribes are, in the first instance, coercive interferences. How liberals deal with interferences that are not expressly coercive depends, among other things, on what they take the liberal project to be and on how they understand "coercion." What follows here will engage these issues only peripherally. For the present purpose, we can take as understood the distinction that Mill (1956) famously drew in the first chapter of *On Liberty* between "remonstrating," "reasoning," "persuading," and "entreating," on the one hand, and "compelling" an individual or "visiting him with (some) evil," on the other. It is the latter category of interferences that liberals are most concerned to regulate.

The idea can be perspicuously described in a contractarian idiom. If we imagine that sovereignty is established by a social contract, then a regime is liberal if the social contract requires individuals to "alienate" only some of the (unlimited) rights they enjoy over themselves in the state of nature. What individuals do not alienate, the sovereign cannot rightfully infringe. John Locke (1690) is a liberal according to this account, because the social contract he envisioned is partial in this sense. Indeed, for Locke and his followers among contemporary libertarians, some rights are literally "inalienable." Hobbes and Rousseau are not liberals; their social contracts are based, as Rousseau (1762) would have it, on "the total alienation by each associate of all his rights." Of course, principled limitations on the use of public coercive force can also be defended without recourse to inalienable rights or social contracts. Thus Mill, a staunch opponent of both rights theory and contractarianism, famously maintained that the principle of utility—or rather his version of it, according to which utility represents "the permanent interests of man as a progressive being"—requires that a certain area of individuals' lives and behaviors be immune from (coercive) public interference of any kind.

Liberals characteristically distinguish the social from the political and maintain that the proper role of political institutions is to superintend a (nonpolitical) civil society. In so doing, they join the tradition in political philosophy that denies that political activity is any part of the good for human beings. In the prototypical, theological version of this political theory, epitomized in the writings of St. Augustine (1950), human beings are said to be so corrupted by Original Sin that no good can come from their own efforts except insofar as they are (unknowingly) directed by providential design. Political institutions exist—in consequence of God's will, not our own—in order to save us from our own destructive natures. They establish order, "the peace of Babylon," allowing for the execution of God's will on earth as humankind advances toward the Final Judgment. They do so, however, in contravention of humanity's fallen nature. Thus they are *unnatural* impositions upon the human race—punishments but also, ironically, because they do substitute order for what would otherwise be a generalized state of mutual antagonism, palliatives for Original Sin.

Needless to say, modern philosophers reject Augustine's theological representations of these positions. But they share the Augustinian view of politics as a necessary evil. Hobbes's example is particularly in point. For Hobbes, the state is concocted by us (not God) to serve our own interests (not God's). But it exists to save us from ourselves and from one another, just as Augustine maintained. The state of nature, the unconstrained expression of human nature, is a "war of all against all." Political institutions therefore conflict with human nature, just as they did for Augustine. Thus they are to be avoided so far as possible. But, given our interests, they cannot be avoided altogether. We are rationally compelled "to seek peace and follow it," and there is no way to do so, Hobbes insisted, except by constructing a "common power," a sovereign "to hold us in awe." This solution to the problem that human beings confront is itself an evil, but a lesser evil than the only feasible alternative in a state of nature, which is to remain locked forever in a war of all against all, to the detriment of everyone's interests.

Contemporary liberals are more sanguine than Augustine or Hobbes about human nature and the prospects for the secular equivalent of "salvation through works," the achievement of worthwhile earthly objectives through uncoerced individual and collective endeavors. But they relegate this possibility to civil society. No good can come from within the political arena—only less bad. This is because states, by their nature, restrict liberty. Thus, like Hobbes, liberals view political institutions as impositions upon individuals. They are *artifices* that force us to do what we would not freely (naturally) do. Society, not the state, is the arena in which self-interested human nature can express itself freely, without giving rise to a devastating war of all against all. But to achieve this end we must first establish a framework that renders self-interest benign and even constructive. This is the mission of the state—its role is to make the world safe for self-interest. Thus, unlike Augustine, liberals do acknowledge the possibility of persons doing well for themselves and for one another through their own efforts. But, like Augustine, they envision no positive role for the state in this endeavor. The state is there only to superintend the arena, outside the state, in which it is safe to leave individuals free to pursue their own conceptions of the good. Thus, in the liberal view, civil society assumes the role that the City of God, outside of time and space, played in Augustine's theology. Liberals do not take Sin or its secular analogue, epitomized in Hobbes's account of human psychology, as seriously as Augustine or Hobbes did. For them, "salvation through works" or rather its secular equivalent, a flourishing civil society, is a human possibility. But liberals share the Augustinian-Hobbesian view of the state as a necessary evil, an imposition upon free beings. Thus, for liberals as for Hobbes, it is desirable to retract the state as much as possible. Hobbes, of course, insisted that, for sovereignty to exist at all, its power must be unrestricted. Hobbes was therefore unable to translate the idea that the state that governs least governs best into a distinctively *liberal* defense of minimal state power. Liberals, on the other hand, make the restriction of political power a matter of principle. Their defining claim has always been that there are things that states may not rightfully do, that certain areas of individuals' lives and behaviors are, as a matter of right, immune from state interference.

It was probably inevitable that the idea of limited sovereignty would be extended from the strictly political realm into the social sphere as well. In this respect, Mill's insistence that "the moral coercion of public opinion" falls as much within the purview of liberal concerns as do state-enforced legal sanctions is emblematic. There is a sense in which this extension of liberalism's defining doctrine does transgress the state/society frontier that played so prominent a role in earlier liberal theory. But it changes nothing with respect to liberalism's affiliation with the Augustinian tradition in political theory. The state is as much a necessary evil for liberals after Mill as it was for earlier liberals or for Hobbes. But the state is no longer the only focus of liberal concern.

The first liberals were strictly proponents of limited government. From Mill's time on, the best liberals have also been defenders of tolerance throughout society at large. Thus, by the mid-nineteenth century, liberalism had become more than just a theory of limited sovereignty. It became a theory of the *good society*. The good society, in the liberal view, is, above all, a tolerant society. The point is not just that liberal states cannot uphold tolerance indefinitely in the face of an intolerant citizenry. Tolerant citizens are indeed indispensable for keeping the state within its proper bounds. But tolerance also makes society better. Thus Mill maintained that a tolerant society encourages human flourishing, while an intolerant society impedes it.

A position is liberal, then, if it marks off an area of individuals' lives and behaviors as immune from state and also societal interference—in other words, if it accords individuals rights against the state and society. In this sense, the received understanding of liberalism is formal, not substantive. What matters is that such rights exist, not what they are. But, in practice, substance is a good proxy for form. Liberal protections characteristically extend to the so-called economic freedoms—the right to hold assets privately, to capitalize on these assets, and to deploy them in production and trade—and to civil liberties like freedom of thought and expression, religious freedom, and the right of assembly. It is a matter of controversy whether economic and civil liberties constitute a seamless web or whether it is possible to support civil liberties without supporting economic freedoms too. However this may be, civil liberties are nowadays defended by all liberal writers, economic freedoms by only some. For all practical purposes, therefore, a concern with protecting speech, religion, assembly, and the like from state and societal interference has become a defining characteristic of liberalism. Even so, it is wise to accede to the received understanding and not define liberalism by the content of the rights it advances. It is then easier to investigate whether some (or perhaps all) of the rights liberals characteristically defend can be justified by appeal to nonliberal or extraliberal reasons.

The idea that liberal protections can indeed be defended in nonliberal ways will be developed in Chapters 4 and 5, where it will emerge that nonliberal justifications for liberal practices are indispensable for the development of defensible supraliberal democratic positions. For now, it will suffice to observe that liberalism is not indispensable for the justification of liberal rights. Thus some contractarian positions that are nonliberal (because they ground political community in a contract of total, not partial, "alienation") provide reasons for supporting at least some traditional (civil) liberties—above all, freedom of thought and expression. Rousseau's theory of sovereignty is a case in point.[1] Just as Mill defended free speech by appealing to its effects on "the permanent interests of man as a progressive being," Rousseau implicitly defended free speech (in the public arena) for instrumental reasons too. If the assemblies of the people are to discover the general will reliably, as they must if individuals are to be free, there cannot be restrictions on the rights of citizens to access or process pertinent information. There must therefore be freedom of thought and expression with respect to everything that bears on public choice. In this respect, Rousseau's account of sovereignty is liberal in its practical implications, even as it is emphatically not a liberal theory. Thus liberal theory is not necessary for grounding liberal practices.

Tolerance and Neutrality

The received understanding of liberalism is *constitutional;* liberalism is a doctrine that proscribes particular state and societal interferences with individuals' lives and behaviors. But liberalism is not just a claim about the limits of the sov-

[1] For further elaboration of this claim, see Levine 1976, 72–80. I would argue, however, that Rousseau's conception of politics, unlike his account of sovereignty, does have illiberal implications. Very generally, Rousseau conceived politics as a timeless struggle for the supremacy of the general will over the private will, a struggle of the "opinion" of citizens. In that struggle, social groups are obstacles in the way of the direct and unmediated general will coordination that legitimates the use of public coercive force. Rousseau therefore assimilated group interests to private interests, placing them on a par, normatively, with the interests of atomic individuals in a state of nature. Thus he proposed that states do whatever must be done to suppress group formation— including proscribing parties and factions, curtailing rights of assembly, instituting censorship, and enforcing a civil religion. These measures undertaken to implement "the exercise of the general will" are, of course, profoundly illiberal, not just in theory but in practice too. I discuss Rousseau's illiberalism at greater length in Levine 1976, 159–86.

ereign's authority. As remarked, it has also come to express a vision of ideal so-cial and political arrangements. Liberals value diversity—in thought, in lifestyle, indeed in all aspects of human endeavor—and encourage tolerance because it promotes diversity. Typically, these aspects of liberal doctrine, its constitutional proscriptions and its positive vision, are integrally joined. Liberalism has there-fore become a philosophy of tolerance. Its watchword is *laissez-vivre.*

Laissez-vivre should not be confused with the economic doctrine of *laissez-faire,* even if some liberals—those who hold that civil and economic liberties comprise a seamless web—believe that the one entails the other. *Laissez-faire* implies reliance on market arrangements and the exclusion of the state from economic affairs—except, of course, to the considerable (and largely unac-knowledged) degree that states are indispensable for maintaining market arrangements. *Laissez-vivre,* on the other hand, implies openness to experimen-tation—in those spheres of life that, according to liberal doctrine, ought to be immune from state and societal interference and also, so far as possible, in areas of human life that the state may rightfully regulate. Thus "tolerance" in liberal theory does not mean quite what it does in ordinary speech. Colloquially, the term suggests forbearance from repressing disapproved ideas and activities, principled passivity. Full-fledged liberal tolerance, on the other hand, implies the active encouragement of diversity and dissent.[2]

This celebration of diversity should not be confused with the homonymous celebration advocated by some "multiculturalists." Their guiding principle ap-pears to be not to offend others, at least not for reasons that have to do with persons' "identities." Liberals do, of course, disparage offensive behavior. Like almost everyone else, they prefer a civil and decorous society to a rancorous one. But liberals are not opposed to giving offense as a matter of constitutional principle. Indeed, in Mill's view, it is wrong to use public coercive force to reg-ulate individuals' behaviors for the sake of preventing offensive behavior. Only the prevention of harm to others justifies such interference.

Rousseau thought that the exercise of the general will is politically feasible only if citizens are "virtuous"—that is, if they are disposed to accord preemi-nence to their interests as "indivisible parts" of "the whole community" and to discount their merely "private" interests accordingly. The dispositions that Rousseau would have institutions instill are therefore generally inimical to *lib-eral* character formation. But liberalism, too, requires institutions to shape indi-viduals' characters to accord with its own agenda. The liberal project is feasible only if citizens are disposed, as it were, "to mind their own business," to respect

---

[2] The difference between the ordinary and technical senses of the term is somewhat diminished if we recognize that what liberals tolerate in the technical sense is diversity and dissent as such, not particular activities, lifestyles or views. Liberals may therefore disapprove of what they actively en-courage. Then they tolerate (in the ordinary sense) what they disapprove of—for the sake of their commitment to tolerance (in the technical sense).

each other's privacy, and, above all, to support an open and experimental social order, even at the cost of encouraging ideas and forms of life of which they disapprove. Just as Rousseauian politics aims at instilling virtue, it is the burden of liberal politics to design and maintain institutions that render persons tolerant.

It is tempting to say that tolerance is a political, not a private, virtue. But, as remarked, it has become commonplace since the mid-nineteenth century to value tolerance between individuals as well as between individuals and the state. It is therefore better to say that tolerance is an interpersonal virtue, not an intrapersonal one. Liberal citizens need be no less partisan, no more noncommittal, than the citizens of any other political order. If they suspend judgment on particular issues or forbear to take sides, it is not for reasons peculiar to the regime under which they live. Liberal states neither encourage nor discourage individual commitment. What tolerance requires is only that people not transgress inappropriately into those areas of other individuals' lives that ought to be immune from interference.

Within their own private spheres, individuals may be as ardent as they please in the pursuit of their own conceptions of the good. Deep commitments and overt partisanship may carry over into the public arena too—subject, however, to constitutional constraints. The state's role is to assure that these rules are observed. But in the end, it is crucial that citizens themselves implement liberal norms. Thus Rawls would have "public reason" guide communal life. Rawls's idea is that in making a case in the public arena, one should not rely upon arguments that are in any way sectarian, even when the positions one is defending are held, in whole or in part, for sectarian reasons. "Public reason," Rawls says, "is the reason of its citizens, of those sharing the status of equal citizenship" (Rawls 1993, 213). Limiting one's argumentative repertoire in this way is especially urgent in societies like our own, where there is dissensus on fundamental moral, philosophical, and religious questions.[3] But reliance on public reason in no way precludes taking sides. There is therefore no reason in principle why, as Robert Frost is supposed to have said, a liberal won't take his own side in an argument (cited in Nagel 1987, 215). Frost's observation of real-world liberals may be apt. But commitment or partisanship is hardly blocked by liberal theory per se.

A useful way to articulate the specifically political aspects of liberal tolerance is to insist that liberalism demands *neutrality*—of intent, not outcome—on the part of public, especially state, institutions (see Chapter 1). As noted, this idea is Rawlsian in inspiration, though Rawls has never quite embraced the term and

---

[3] I will discuss the nature of this purported dissensus and its implications presently. In recent years, public reason has occupied the attention of many of Rawls's followers and (sympathetic) critics. For a useful account of some problems, see Weinstock 1994.

has lately distanced himself from it expressly (see Rawls 1993, 190–95). The idea is emblematic, however, of political liberalism, broadly construed.

It should be pointed out that in the essay that launched the term "neutrality" into contemporary discussions, Ronald Dworkin (1978) was less concerned with defending tolerance per se than with bringing to light certain affinities between liberal political philosophy and liberal politics as it is understood in the United States and similarly minded political cultures. Dworkin took the post–New Deal conception of liberal politics, with its (partial) commitment to state interventions against institutional factors that disable individuals from exercising formal liberties, as a paradigm, as one of a number of distinctively liberal "settlements" that have coalesced over the past two centuries. He argued that New Deal social policies express a "constitutive political morality" that supplies a particular interpretation to the (broadly Kantian) idea that persons are free and equal moral agents, worthy of equal respect. By analyzing this last great liberal settlement, Dworkin concluded that a position is liberal if it upholds the moral equality of persons by precluding the use of public coercive force to favor individuals' particular conceptions of the good. Thus, in Dworkin's view, New Deal liberalism expresses this underlying "essence" in its policy prescriptions by articulating what neutrality requires under the particular historical conditions that existed at the time of its emergence and tenure. In earlier times, liberalism's constitutive political morality underwrote different political measures. And, of course, in conditions that did not exist at the time of past liberal settlements, liberals would be obliged to advocate yet unprecedented institutional arrangements. It was in this spirit that I argued that there is a liberal case for sufficiently affluent societies according individuals an unconditional right not to work, a right that no liberal society has ever bestowed.

It is plain that Dworkin's account of neutrality was significantly influenced by Rawls's contention, implicit in *A Theory of Justice* and developed expressly in papers written shortly thereafter, that principles of justice ought to treat rival conceptions of the good fairly (see, for example, Rawls 1975). However, Rawls's aim, at least in his writings of the past two decades, is orthogonal to Dworkin's. He is not intent on explicating liberalism's constitutive political morality, and I would venture that he has no serious quarrel with Dworkin's account of neutrality. Rawls's principal concern in *Political Liberalism* is political legitimacy. His aim is to justify neutrality, and to do so in a way that is itself distinctively liberal.[4] Thus Rawls would effectively wrest neutrality (the idea, not the term) away from moral philosophy. Important moral philosophical positions—Mil-

---

[4] Larmore (1987), following some early indications of the position that emerges in *Political Liberalism,* seeks to provide "neutral" justifications for neutral political arrangements. In *Political Liberalism,* however, it is plain that Rawls has no illusions about the prospects for justificatory arguments that appeal to no contentious underlying convictions whatever.

lian and Kantian liberalism, for example—do endorse neutrality on the part of public institutions. But Rawls would not have support for neutrality depend upon the truth of these (or any other) "comprehensive doctrines."[5] Rather, he would defend neutrality by garnering support for constitutional principles that have this effect, principles that proponents of different comprehensive doctrines, liberal or otherwise, can all endorse.

Rawls's account of political legitimacy is importantly ambiguous—in consequence of the fact that throughout *Political Liberalism* he conflates a very striking and original account of de jure legitimacy (legitimacy in right) with questions about political stability and other issues that bear on the de facto legitimacy of political arrangements. Political arrangements are de facto legitimate if they are believed to be legitimate by most of the people they affect; in contrast, de jure legitimacy can exist (or not) irrespective of citizens' beliefs about it. In what follows, I mainly address Rawls's account of de jure legitimacy. But it will sometimes be necessary to accede to the ambiguity of Rawls's own discussion and not distinguish these issues carefully. It is in this spirit that I scrutinize Rawls's contention that (most) people in societies like our own can in fact be brought to endorse constitutional principles that insure neutrality on the part of public institutions.

Because it is supposed to follow from an (imputed) consensus that could fail to exist, political liberalism is not a universally applicable political philosophy. In Rawls's version, it makes no claim to "metaphysical" truth.[6] Thus we cannot say that political institutions should uphold neutrality in all times and places. In fact, political liberalism, as Rawls conceives it, is almost certainly not defensible in all circumstances. Rawls's claim is only that support for liberal constitutional principles is possible and desirable in the conditions that actually obtain in generally liberal societies. There is no political liberalism, therefore, that will pass muster "under the aspect of eternity." The claim is only that the doctrine is right *for us now* and, of course, for anyone else similarly situated.

It is evidently Rawls's intent that individuals enthusiastically support neutral political institutions. Political liberalism therefore suggests a political project:

[5] A *comprehensive doctrine* "includes conceptions of what is of value in human life, and ideals of personal character, as well as ideals of friendship and of familial and associational relationships, and much else that is to inform our conduct and in the limit to our life as a whole. A conception is fully comprehensive if it covers all recognized values and virtues within one rather precisely articulated system; whereas a conception is only partially comprehensive when it comprises a number of, but by no means all, nonpolitical values and virtues and is rather loosely articulated" (Rawls 1993, 13).

[6] But neither is Rawls committed to the kind of relativism that would deny that there are "metaphysical" truths, such as those to which political philosophers have traditionally appealed. His claim is only that political philosophy per se need not and should not appeal to such truths, at least in the conditions that obtain in well-functioning liberal democracies in the late twentieth century. Metaphysics divides; political liberalism, as Rawls conceives it, aims to unite.

to secure such support. The actual should be made to conform to the ideal. Rawls would pursue this objective by building an "overlapping consensus." An overlapping consensus contrasts with a "modus vivendi," an agreement to get along in the face of otherwise contentious disputes over fundamental values. A modus vivendi is too fragile a basis for social unity and stability; among other things, it is prone to become undone as the balance of forces within a society changes. The aim therefore is to base support for neutrality on convictions actively endorsed throughout the political community. But except for those citizens whose comprehensive doctrines are expressly liberal, support for neutrality is, at best, only latent. The task, then, is to make it manifest, to develop backing for the constitutional order by appealing to elements already present in the comprehensive doctrines individuals hold. This task will, of course, be easier if individuals are already won over to philosophical positions that uphold neutrality directly. But it is not necessary, for this project to succeed, that individuals actually be philosophical liberals. What is necessary is only that the comprehensive doctrines they endorse not fall beyond the range of a potential overlapping consensus around liberal constitutional principles. If there is insufficient "overlap," coercion, not consensus, would be the only conceivable means for assuring the stability of governing structures. Rawls is confident, however, that the requisite consensus does exist in principle. In consequence of the cultural and political transformations wrought by the Protestant Reformation, the Enlightenment, and the history of liberalism itself, an overlapping consensus is there to be forged.

To repeat, the kind of neutrality that is envisioned in a liberal constitutional regime is neutrality of intent, not of effect. In even the most austerely neutral regimes, some conceptions of the good will prevail over others. No sane liberal would expect otherwise or seek to undo the inevitable. But even at the level of intent, it is plain that a state dedicated to implementing neutrality can never be quite so "neutral" as the word suggests. Liberal states can accommodate nonliberal comprehensive doctrines if they are compatible with a constitutional order that tolerates diverse conceptions of the good. But expressly antiliberal positions are a different matter. Thus no state could be expected to treat literally all (imaginable) conceptions of the good equally. If nothing else, liberal states cannot be neutral with respect to practices or activities that would undo their own neutrality. Nor can liberal states be neutral with respect to ways of life that undermine the moral equality of persons, even if they are part of individuals' comprehensive doctrines. Thus it is fair to conclude that liberal states can rightfully prohibit slavery, whether or not slavery is permissible according to some religious or secular worldview. Other practices that similarly reinforce systematic inequalities may also be candidates for proscription. Certain forms of prostitution or commercial (gestational) surrogacy may be examples (see, for example, Satz 1992, 1995). Neutrality applies to whatever upholds, or at least does not undermine, the moral equality of persons. Within that range, liberals insist that state power not be used to favor some conceptions of the good over others. But even with this restriction in force, liberalism is a demanding doctrine. Thus we saw in Chapter 1 that a commitment to neutrality has implications far-reaching enough to challenge some settled intuitions of most people, including most liberals, in our political culture.

Deeds are one thing, words another. Liberals generally hold states to the strictest neutrality with respect to speech opposed to the constitutional order. Indeed, if Mill is right, the advocacy of subversive views can actually advance the liberal project (Mill 1956, chap. 2). There is the possibility, for one thing, that subversive speech is true or partly true. But even if it is utterly without merit, there are still good consequentialist reasons to allow it and even to encourage its promulgation. "The lively collision of truth with error" is always salutary, Mill believed, in preventing settled convictions from degenerating into dogmas and, above all, in fostering the moral and intellectual capacities that are indispensable if liberal tolerance is to work its beneficial effects. Moreover, the risks of tolerance are minimal in regimes where order is secured by a rational consensus. Thus there is little reason to fear that speech, any speech, will undermine the prevailing constitutional order of a well-governed liberal state. Other liberals defend free speech on different grounds—for example, for its role in maintaining and enhancing autonomy (see, for example, Scanlon 1972; Redish 1982; Strauss 1991). But there is a general consensus that while there may be something to fear from antiliberal deeds, so long as all is well in the polity, even the most subversive words should be vigorously protected.

Finally, as remarked, there are always unintended consequences of legitimate state activities that advance some conceptions of the good at the expense of others—especially in regimes organized in accord with liberal settlements that imply an activist role for state institutions. Public provision of a right not to work is a case in point: such a right is inimical to many, indeed most, extant conceptions of the good, but it is defensible on liberal grounds nevertheless. Paradoxically, too, some conceptions of the good are bound to prevail over others in consequence of the exercise of neutrality itself. Thus a neutral state could not employ state power to oppose, say, religious liberty or the right of a woman to an abortion—despite the fact that illiberal conceptions of the good (conceptions that imply religious intolerance or oppose reproductive freedom) exist among the comprehensive doctrines that Rawls would organize into an overlapping consensus. Where neutrality reigns, tolerance is the default position. Conceptions of the good in which tolerance is a preeminent value will therefore always prevail over those that would enforce conceptions of the good upon others.

Social Unity

As remarked, it is not always possible to disentangle Rawls's account of de jure political legitimacy from his views on actually existing beliefs and their effects on social stability. But to the extent that it is possible to do so, it is fair to say that Rawls's account of de jure legitimacy appeals to stability or order to a degree that is unusual even for liberals. In this respect, Rawls appears to agree with Hobbes, the preeminent proponent of stability and order. Hobbes, however, was for order irrespective of the regime in place. In his view, the most likely alternative to the status quo, whatever it might be, is a devastating "war of all against all," a condition to be avoided at all costs. To avert this outcome, Hobbes would have the state suppress whatever is potentially disruptive of social order, including all but the most tepid political opposition. A tolerant regime would incur unreasonable (and unnecessary) risks. Political liberals, however, value dissent. They are able to do so and still accord stability and order the importance they do because, unlike Hobbes, they see little merit in order for its own sake. When they appeal to the importance of social stability, it is not for the sake of order per se but for the sake of the values liberalism serves. Thus they value social stability *in liberal polities* but not necessarily elsewhere. Political liberals living in nonliberal regimes could therefore be rebels or even revolutionaries, in contravention of the fundamentally conservative and anti-revolutionary thrust of Hobbesian politics (see Ackerman 1994).

There is a more pertinent respect, however, in which political liberals are not Hobbesians. Hobbes would establish order by fear. People obey the sovereign because they fear his police. Liberals, including political liberals, do not entirely disagree. They are not anarchists. Like Hobbes, they believe that a state is indispensable for coordinating individuals' behaviors. But they seek to minimize coercion. Thus, so far as possible, they would substitute willing support for the regime for fear of its repressive power. They would have individuals accede to "the rules of the game" because they want to do so, not because they fear the consequences of noncompliance. Social division is inimical to this desideratum. Social unity is therefore a paramount liberal aim.

As such, social unity is, simultaneously, a condition for the possibility of liberal regimes and a goal of liberal politics. Thus it functions very much as Mill thought tolerance does. In Mill's view, a certain level of tolerance is necessary before tolerance can have beneficial effects. Beyond that threshold, however, the more tolerance there is, the more beneficial tolerance becomes. Similarly, a consensus in support of liberal constitutional measures presupposes a threshold level of social unity. When it exists, there can be well-functioning liberal institutions that, in turn, foster social unity, reinforcing the condition for their own possibility. They foster unity by mitigating conflicts that threaten to exacerbate social divisions, conflicts that deliberative political institutions, insofar as they exist, are unable to address. Thus liberal constitutional provisions—especially those that exist in the United States, the exemplars for Rawls and other political liberals—aim to transform (most) political disagreements into legal disputes. There is, of course, a place for public deliberation and collective choice in liberal democracies. But it is not a large place (see Chapter 4). For political liberals, at least implicitly, the aim is to have most conflicts settled "administratively"—by the proper application of "the rules of the game," adjudicated by a judicial or extrajudicial administrative system insulated from political pressures. Thus the fear of the sovereign's police that Hobbes sought to instill gives way, in the liberal vision, to a system that insures order by according dominion to law itself. For this system to sustain itself, it must have the loyalty of its subjects. There must be a significant degree of support for its basic institutional arrangements or, in other words, a substantial measure of social unity. Then overt coercion, which all liberals seek to minimize, can be reduced. At the limit, it need only be deployed against recalcitrants. To be sure, the system in place still rests ultimately on the use or threat of force; the state is a necessary condition for the rule of law. But what keeps a war of all against all at bay is not so much the repressive apparatus that makes the rule of law possible, but respect for the law itself and the institutions upon which it is based.

By keeping this objective in mind, it is possible to reconstruct Rawls's position in a way that partially disentangles his accounts of de jure and de facto legitimacy. Rawls wants widespread acceptance of the de facto legitimacy of liberal institutions to be based upon the fact that these institutions really are legitimate, that they are legitimate de jure. But at the same time Rawls insists that in a generally free society many different comprehensive doctrines will have adherents, and some of these comprehensive doctrines will be non- or even antiliberal. In these circumstances, what is a political liberal to do? The answer is plain: the requisite consensus, insofar as it is not already manifest, must be forged—not through coercion but through rational persuasion. Is this possible? The conviction that motivates the political liberal project is that indeed it is. If it is not, then the political liberal's account of de jure political legitimacy will fail. It is not enough to show that legitimate authority is conceivable; one must also demonstrate that the concept has some possible applicability in our time and place.

Rawls's strategy is this: begin with extant and ostensibly opposing comprehensive doctrines, some of which may be officially illiberal; find higher-order commitments that proponents of all of these views endorse; and then, so far as possible, derive a consensus supporting liberal constitutional arrangements on the basis of these higher-order commitments. The foundational commitments that Rawls identifies are, in fact, relatively uncontentious: that persons are morally equal in possessing capacities for a sense of justice and for a conception of the good, and also that people have rational capacities for judgment, thought, and inference. But even in *Political Liberalism*, where the notion of an overlapping consensus is extensively developed, Rawls asserts—rather than actually demonstrates—his claim that a consensus on individuals' moral powers and rational capacities entails support for neutrality on the part of public institutions, that is, fairness to competing conceptions of the good. Rawls nowhere *shows* how an overlapping consensus can be forged out of actual comprehensive doctrines. What he does instead is adduce (generally inconclusive) considerations in support of the claim that a particular subset of extant positions, the "reasonable" ones, can be dialectically shaped into a consensus of the requisite sort. Insofar as "reasonable" is defined independently, so that it is not true by definition that "reasonable" comprehensive doctrines support liberal constitutional principles (at least implicitly), this conviction is an empirical speculation, not an incontrovertible fact. Evidently, Rawls and other political liberals believe that in generally free societies, many (if not most) comprehensive doctrines will in fact be reasonable. Otherwise, liberal institutions might survive— through fear or indifference on the part of the citizenry—but a well-ordered, flourishing liberal state would remain an elusive ideal.

Neutrality with respect to "unreasonable" comprehensive doctrines is a luxury that can be supported so long as the likely harm done to liberal regimes is negligible. In flourishing liberal polities, tolerance even of potentially subversive practices and activities is, as noted, harmless and perhaps even salutary. If nothing else, it helps to foster the habit of toleration. *Unreasonable* comprehensive doctrines are, so to speak, resident aliens among the views that, upon re-description, constitute the overlapping consensus Rawls aims to achieve. Accordingly, their "rights" are conditional to some extent on the ability of the larger society to accommodate them. Reasonable comprehensive doctrines, on the other hand, qualify for full citizenship.

If we say, following Plato, that the virtue of a thing is that which allows it to perform its function well, then, there is an emerging body of liberal theory that maintains that reasonableness is the first virtue of political liberalism, just as tolerance itself was the first virtue of Millian liberal theory.[7] But "reasonable" is, at best, a vague term, especially applied to comprehensive doctrines.[8] I think it is

---

[7] See Wolff 1968, 122–23. On the virtue of reasonableness, see, for example, Rawls 1987, 1989, 1993; Cohen 1990; Gutmann 1993.

[8] Even Rawls (1993, 59) agrees that it is "deliberately loose." This characterization follows his most extensive gloss on the idea: "Reasonable comprehensive doctrines . . . have three main features. One is that a reasonable doctrine is an exercise of theoretical reason: it covers the major religious, philosophical, and moral aspects of human life in a more or less consistent and coherent manner. It organizes and characterizes recognized values so that they are compatible with one another and express an intelligible view of the world. Each doctrine will do this in ways that distinguish it from other doctrines, for example, by giving certain values a particular primacy and weight. In singling out which values to count as especially significant and how to balance them when they conflict, a reasonable comprehensive doctrine is also an exercise of practical reason. . . . Finally, a third feature is that while a reasonable comprehensive doctrine is not necessarily fixed and unchanging, it normally belongs to, or draws upon, a tradition of thought and doctrine. Although stable over time, and not subject to sudden and unexplained changes, it tends to evolve slowly in the light of what, from its point of view, it sees as good and sufficient conditions."

also an ambiguous idea. On the one hand, a position or comprehensive doctrine is reasonable if it can be modified or at least redescribed in a way that makes cooperation with others who hold different views possible on free and equal terms. "Reasonable" in this sense means "flexible" or "cooperative." On the other hand, a position or comprehensive doctrine is reasonable if it is plausible, given the uncertainties that inevitably afflict human deliberations. On this view, disagreements with respect to fundamental religious or moral issues are reasonable so long as their existence cannot be explained by the willful or inadvertent blindness or irrationality of one or another side. "The burdens and uncertainties that afflict any conscientious use of rational powers under real world conditions—shortage of time, lack of conclusive evidence, difficulty in prioritizing values" make a range of conflicting and even incommensurable views reasonable in this sense (Waldron 1993, 5). Rawls insists that reasonable disagreements, so understood, are permanent and ineradicable features of modern societies. The expectation that fundamental moral, philosophical, and religious differences will eventually disappear is therefore itself unreasonable (in the sense that contrasts with "plausible"). Rawls is therefore quite liberal (in the colloquial sense of "broadminded" or "generous") in what he deems reasonable. Most extant moral, philosophical, and religious doctrines meet his standard.

But can this understanding be sustained? How can we say, for example, that someone is reasonable who believes in the existence of an omnipotent, omniscient, and perfectly good God when that person also believes that there are no considerations that weigh in favor of the existence of such a being and many that weigh against? Is it reasonable to believe in what one considers absurd or, as some theists are wont, to believe in God *because* the belief is absurd? Political liberals would surely say yes; without exception, they classify at least mainstream religious beliefs in the reasonable category, irrespective of the creedal states of believers. But how can we find reasonable what we believe to be false and/or unworthy of serious consideration (even if it is not wildly delusional)? Rawls's answer is that if we are aware of "the burdens of deliberation," we can come to understand, despite our own convictions, that human beings can in good faith arrive at positions contrary to our own. But is this always so? Surely it matters why we think a belief is false or not worth taking seriously. It is relevant that many of the beliefs upon which comprehensive doctrines rest can be reasonably (plausibly) dismissed for reasons that, if believed, swamp any reasonable (appropriate) sensitivity to the burdens of judgment. Thus, on Freud's account (1927), theistic convictions bear profound affinities with certain neuroses and arise from the same causal mechanisms. More specifically, the belief in God is an "illusion," an expression of an unconscious wish, in just the way that, to use Freud's analogy, a middle-class girl's belief that a prince will come to marry her is. Thus Freud expressly denied that theistic beliefs are delusional; they are not held in the face of overwhelming evidence to the contrary—as would be the case, for example, if this girl were to believe that she is Cleopatra.

Is the belief that a prince will come therefore reasonable? In answering this question, it is relevant to take into account not only the improbability of what is believed, but also the nature of the mechanism that accounts for it. Given the probabilities and the illusional character of the belief itself, it is hard to see how anyone, even the most dedicated political liberal, could call the belief that a prince will come reasonable. But Freud's point is that the same mechanism—and the same improbability—afflicts theistic belief. Whether or not he was right, this example makes clear the fatal indeterminacy of "reasonableness" in the political liberal's lexicon. Those who think Freud right but nevertheless support the reasonableness of comprehensive doctrines like Christianity or Judaism are, one suspects, guilty (perhaps inadvertently) of a conceptual slight of hand: identifying the "reasonable" with what they think ought to be protected from societal and state interference. They are, in other words, confounding the policy they want with the justification they provide. A Freudian atheist—or an adherent of any of a host of complementary or rival social or psychological theories that come to similar conclusions about theism—could endorse the policy recommendation liberals proffer; they could defend freedom of religion. But they could hardly do so for the reason Rawls advances: that theistic beliefs can be plausibly entertained in light of the burdens of judgment.

It is plain, in any case, that what is reasonable in light of the burdens of judgment, even on Rawls's expansive understanding of the idea, need not also be reasonable in the sense of flexible or cooperative, and vice versa. Rawls effectively blurs the line between these senses of "reasonable" by saying that a view is held reasonably only if its proponents recognize the hopelessness of trying to convert everybody to it. The idea, it seems, is that people will moderate their claims for the sake of social cooperation whenever they acknowledge the futility of defeating conflicting or incommensurable comprehensive doctrines noncoercively—through the force of argument or, where arguments fail, through extrarational forms of persuasion that are not illiberal. The contrast is with scientific communities in which a consensus around basic theoretical orientations is a fair expectation, at least for those "hard" sciences that are theoretically mature and relatively insulated from political and religious pressures. Rawls's conviction, apparently, is that fundamental moral, philosophical, and religious differences can never be surmounted, unlike fundamental scientific differences which, when they occur, are temporary phenomena that the progress of science will eventually resolve (Rawls 1993, 55).

To assume this contrast, it is not necessary to suppose that scientific theories develop continuously, propelled along by a universally acknowledged and incontrovertible "scientific method." Hopes for a rational consensus in the sciences are even compatible with the well-known view of Thomas S. Kuhn (1962), according to which fundamental changes of theoretical orientation, "paradigm shifts," seldom if ever result from the force of new evidence or theoretical argumentation alone. Following Kuhn's metaphor, science changes through "scientific revolutions" in which new and even incommensurable theories arise on the ashes of old paradigms, when new scientific communities or new strata within existing scientific communities supplant practitioners of old orthodoxies. In consequence of the (largely extrarational) means through which old regimes are overthrown and replaced, a new consensus is forged in which fundamental differences eventually recede. Agreement is achieved, not so much because it is rationally necessitated, though it generally is retrospectively, but because it is politically implemented. Even so, scientific revolutionaries seldom, if ever, rely on expressly illiberal means to achieve agreement. And in any case, scientific revolutions are relatively brief discontinuities that punctuate the history of successive forms of "normal science" in which rational consensus is the norm. But if Rawls is right, there is no similar prospect for the comprehensive doctrines that populate the intellectual and moral landscape of modern, liberal societies, no likelihood of a rational consensus emerging within the community at large. Liberals therefore cannot rely on the ordinary course of events to foster social unity. It is Rawls's contention, however, that in the absence of an overt consensus around constitutional principles for mediating potential conflicts, liberal institutions themselves would be in peril. In those circumstances, so long as people care intensely about the (sometimes conflicting) comprehensive doctrines they support, order can only be imposed by force, in contravention of liberalism's basic rationale. Hence the need to *forge* an overlapping consensus around constitutional principles that uphold neutrality as a principled conviction.

If the issue was just de facto legitimacy, Rawls's account would seem exaggerated at best. Contemporary liberal democracies are no longer riven by the threat of religious or civil war. If anything, indifference about comprehensive doctrines, not fanatical adherence, has become the norm. But again, despite his own equivocations, Rawls's claims in behalf of an overlapping consensus of reasonable comprehensive doctrines pertain mainly to the problem of de jure, not de facto, legitimacy. The issue is not so much what is necessary for civil peace as what is required to legitimate the use of public coercive force.

I will argue presently that, even so, Rawls's depiction of the problem political liberals confront is misleading. But it is worth noting, first, that an overlapping consensus is not the only solution to the problem Rawls formulates. A sense of the reasonableness of a comprehensive doctrine, of its plausibility in light of "the burdens of judgment," may sometimes incline its opponents to accommodate to it. But a recognition of the futility of attempts at persuading followers of one comprehensive doctrine to "convert" to another can follow as much from a belief in the irrationality of one's fellow citizens as from an appreciation of the reasonableness (plausibility) of their views. Thus the Freudian atheist may be as confident of the impossibility of converting religious fundamentalists to a broadly secular theoretical orientation as any political liberal is. Even more in point, there are grounds for supporting liberal norms that have nothing to do with the improbability of reaching a consensus on comprehensive doctrines. Recall, for example, Mill's reason for allowing even manifestly false ideas into the public arena—his claim that the "collision . . . [of truth] with error" is a powerful means for cultivating the moral and intellectual capacities that are indispensable if tolerance is to have beneficial effects.

Rawls maintains nevertheless that only an overlapping consensus will do. Otherwise, he insists, the best we can hope for is a modus vivendi, which he deems an insufficient basis for social unity. Perhaps he is right, if a modus vivendi is understood as an armed truce, a cessation of hostilities undertaken to avoid what would otherwise be a generalized state of war (Rawls 1993, 147). But endorsement of social cooperation in the manner Rawls prescribes and grudging acceptance of diversity are not the only ways to arrive at social cooperation on liberal terms. That they might appear to be is an artifact, I believe, of an equivocation at the heart of political liberalism. For Rawls and other political liberals, political liberalism is an "ideal theory," and therein lies an important ambiguity.

Ideal Theory

For Rawls, a theory is ideal if it assumes full compliance. The contrast is with partial compliance theories, which represent situations in which (some) institutions and persons remain recalcitrant to the theory's demands.[9] I will use the term in a related but more colloquial sense—to designate visions of ideal (but feasible) social and political arrangements. Because political liberalism is an ideal theory in the latter sense, it is *political* in a way that political liberals seldom acknowledge.

For political liberals, political liberalism is political in the sense that it is not itself a comprehensive doctrine but a theory of political legitimacy—one that purports to resolve allegedly intractable disagreements about fundamental human commitments in a political way, reconciling differences through a kind of negotiation. As such, its defenders claim, it enhances the stability of liberal states to a degree that the "metaphysical" liberalisms with which it contrasts cannot. I will comment presently on the plausibility of this contention. For now, I want only to register an observation about the political implications of the political liberal's belief that this claim is true. Political liberals, like liberals generally, support a style of politics that stresses continuity with received practices and institutional arrangements—provided, again, that the institutions in place are already substantially liberal. Thus their politics (in the colloquial sense) is *liberal,* not radical or revolutionary. But because political liberalism puts social unity at the center of its account of political legitimacy—because it is

---

[9] On Rawls's usage, see Rawls 1971, 8–9; Waldron 1994, 379–80.

committed, in consequence, to the indefinite perpetuation of constitutional procedures more or less like those already in place in liberal democracies like the United States—it is tied conceptually to existing institutional arrangements in a way that other liberalisms are not. Thus it poses more of an obstacle to the development of a theory and practice *beyond* liberalism than these rival liberalisms do.

Because they were critics of the existing order, radicals of the left often used to evince hostility toward liberal politics even to the point of eschewing tolerance itself. Whatever they may have considered the role of tolerance to be under ideal conditions, the actual world, in their view, fell so far short of the ideal that illiberal political styles could sometimes be apt. I argue in Chapters 4 and 5 that this conclusion is too hasty and that what contemporary egalitarians should retrieve from the radical traditions that brought forth and sustained egalitarian aspirations in the past is not their illiberalism but their vision of what ideal social and political arrangements can be. My position, therefore, is the inverse of the usual one. It is not that the politics of political liberals is faulty on the grounds that the actual political situation in liberal polities differs more profoundly from political liberalism's ideal theory than political liberals acknowledge. I will not call for illiberal means to achieve liberal or supraliberal ends. My claim instead is that liberalism's ideal theory is flawed or, at least, damagingly limited. Liberal politics probably is apt for our time and place. There are aspects of it that are likely to remain apt for an indefinite future. But, to its detriment, political liberalism is wedded to existing liberal politics in ways that other liberalisms are not. Even more than some of the liberalisms it purports to supplant, political liberalism blocks progress toward a more genuinely egalitarian future.

I should emphasize, finally, that, in making this claim, it is political liberalism, not liberal egalitarian justice, that I am taking to task. I will argue eventually that a truly egalitarian society would be a society largely *beyond* justice. But even on this side of that state of affairs, it is an open question what kinds of institutional arrangements or political practices justice requires. Rawlsian justice is a case in point. Despite all the attention that has been lavished on the subject, it is far from clear how best to implement the principles of justice Rawls identifies.[10] Thus it is possible, Rawls's own beliefs notwithstanding, that under real world conditions, Rawlsian justice entails a political practice that radically

[10] One might be tempted to read Rawls's first principle of justice, that basic rights and liberties be distributed equally and to the greatest extent possible, as a requirement that political institutions must be liberal or, rather, liberal democratic—in other words, that they recognize equality of citizenship in the way that liberal democracies do. Then, contrary to what I have just claimed, Rawlsian justice *would* directly block efforts to transcend liberal horizons. The account of liberal democracy that I offer in Chapter 4 will implicitly challenge this reading. At this point, I would only suggest that Rawls's insistence that basic rights and liberties be accorded their "fair value" raises more questions than it settles—not only about the economic structure of a just society but also about its fundamental political institutions.

challenges the last liberal settlement, its descendant practices and institutions, and indeed any likely future configuration of liberal positions. Rawls does not so much dispute as ignore this possibility. He does insist that the principal positions set forth in *A Theory of Justice* cohere with the account of political legitimacy developed in *Political Liberalism* and the writings that precede it, thereby suggesting that the politics implicit in the two books are the same.[11] I will not gainsay this impression overall. But I would observe that Rawls is prepared to acknowledge the legitimacy of societies that fail to accord with his principles of justice. He would even be obliged to agree that societies that seek to implement rival views—utilitarian theories, for example—could be legitimate. In short, Rawlsian justice is a more demanding requirement than Rawlsian political legitimacy. I submit that this is not the only respect in which these components of Rawls's liberalism differ. Political liberalism, the less demanding theory, pulls in a different direction than the theory of justice. Rawlsian justice has radically redistributive implications. Political liberalism, on the other hand, is self-consciously dedicated to stabilizing the status quo of liberal regimes. It is a conservative doctrine.

Instrumental Liberalism

For Mill, tolerance of thought and expression, of experiments in living, and of individuals' behaviors generally is justified because, in his view, its consequences for "the permanent interests of man as a progressive being" are better than the consequences of any less tolerant social policy. Thus Mill defends liberalism instrumentally. He does so, moreover, in the name of a comprehensive doctrine, a version of utilitarianism. Is his defense of liberal institutions therefore flawed, as political liberals believe? I think the answer is no. Instrumental liberalism is not inferior to political liberalism—at the level of ideal theory. If this conclusion can be sustained, and if it is in fact the case that instrumental liberalism is more conducive to egalitarian objectives than its more contemporary rival, then it would follow that inasmuch as liberalism is still crucial to the realization of the goals that motivate egalitarians, egalitarians ought to be instrumental, not political, liberals.

It is important to realize that the nature of liberal institutions themselves is not in dispute. Millian (or Kantian) liberals are as committed to tolerance as political liberals are. Thus there is a sense in which what distinguishes political liberalism from instrumental liberalism does not matter—in practice. To the degree that the stability of liberal regimes is at issue, however, there may nevertheless be some practical respects in which political liberalism and instrumental liberalism differ. I will speculate on these differences presently. But they too are

[11] In support of this view, see Estlund 1996.

largely irrelevant to the question at hand. As noted, Rawls and other political liberals sometimes confound questions of de facto and de jure legitimacy. This confusion comes to a head when social stability is at issue. In order to make the case that there is no need on this account for instrumental liberalism to give way to political liberalism, it will be necessary, once again, to follow Rawls onto his own terrain, equivocal as it may be. Ultimately, though, it is de jure legitimacy that is in contention. Political liberals maintain that any instrumental liberal theory of de jure legitimacy must fail to respect the moral equality of persons—because instrumental liberalism is only one of a number of reasonable, but still contentious, comprehensive doctrines. I will argue that they are wrong to insist that instrumental liberalism ought to be rejected for this reason.

First, though, with respect to social stability, it is important to realize that a modus vivendi of the sort Rawls deplores is not the only alternative to the overlapping consensus he defends. It might at first appear that there are no alternatives, for if tolerance is to be defended instrumentally, there would have to be some end or set of ends for which it is instrumental. These ends will be vulnerable to rejection for reasons that we all would be obliged to find reasonable in light of the burdens of judgment. Very likely, therefore, some citizens will reject these ends. Social unity would then diminish and the stability of the regime would decline accordingly. This argument is plausible at the level of generality at which it is pitched. But that degree of abstraction conveys a misleading impression; for the values to which instrumental liberals appeal are so widely shared that it is fair to speculate that a consensus around them would be nearly as broad as the overlapping consensus Rawls envisions. Nearly everyone whom political liberals would be able to bring into an overlapping consensus should be susceptible to being won over to instrumental liberalism too. If political liberalism is at an advantage in this regard, it is a vanishingly small advantage, too slight to register significantly.

What political liberals claim is that any "metaphysical" justification of liberal institutional arrangements is bound to command less support than an overlapping consensus encompassing metaphysically liberal positions and other nonliberal comprehensive doctrines as well. On the face of it, this is true. But this truth would matter only if a commitment to advancing "the permanent interests of man as a progressive being" (Mill) or to "treating persons as ends and never as means only" (Kant) would in fact be inimical to a significant number of "reasonable" citizens of liberal states. Ultimately, this is an empirical question on which we can only speculate. My claim is that the relevant metaphysical liberalisms are likely to enlist nearly as much support directly as can be garnered through the program that political liberals advocate. To speculate otherwise, one would have to ignore the content of the liberalisms in contention and assimilate them, without reason, to a category that encompasses the entire range of reasonable (not "wildly irrational") comprehensive doctrines. This is just what political liberals do. They imagine that being "metaphysical" (in contrast to "political") makes a theory needlessly contentious. But this is not so, as can be easily shown. I will focus on metaphysical liberalisms of the Millian kind— that is, on instrumental liberalism—because I believe that this strain of liberal theory is, in fact, the most conducive to egalitarian aims. But as far as the de facto legitimacy of liberal regimes is a concern, many of the same considerations would surely apply to other metaphysical liberalisms as well.

Political liberals may be right when they insist that there will always be fundamental disagreements about comprehensive doctrines in free societies. They may be right as well when they maintain that some of these disagreements, though probably not as many as they imagine, are reasonable (irresolvable in light of the burdens of judgment). But they do not accept that there can be—indeed, there already is—a consensus around certain core values, not only in liberal societies but virtually everywhere today. It is plain that, at a level of abstraction that overlooks differences in emphasis and idiosyncrasies of usage, nearly everyone does in fact endorse the values instrumental liberalism prizes above all others—autonomy and self-realization.

This is, of course, a conjecture, just as is Rawls's belief in the stability enhancing consequences of an overlapping consensus of reasonable comprehensive doctrines. Rawls's position is indeed weaker in the sense that the consensus he would forge is based on more general and therefore less contentious claims than the commitments that instrumental liberals expressly endorse. In Rawls's view, the idea that human beings are somewhat rational and that they possess fundamental moral powers—they exercise a sense of justice and hold a conception of the good—suffice for constructing an overlapping consensus. But this ostensible advantage is also potentially a shortcoming; for it remains to be demonstrated that reasonable comprehensive doctrines, assuming they can somehow be identified unproblematically, all do converge around support for liberal constitutionalism. Thus the claim that there exists an overlapping consensus of reasonable comprehensive doctrines is problematic—partly in consequence of the fact that the prior consensus on which it is based is so weak. On the other hand, there is no doubt that instrumental liberalism underwrites liberal institutional arrangements. But whatever the prospects for the political liberal idea may be, my claim is only that autonomy and self-realization are so widely valued—by metaphysical liberals, of course, and by many nonliberals as well—that the a priori stability advantages of an overlapping consensus are effectively wiped out. If I am right, and insofar as the issue in contention is the stability of liberal regimes, then even if the political liberal project can be made to succeed in the way Rawls assumes, the contest between political and instrumental liberalism would effectively come to a draw.

My point is not just that there are already sufficient numbers of metaphysical liberals in existing political communities to render a Rawlsian overlapping consensus superfluous for assuring social stability. Rather it is that the deepest valuational commitments of instrumental liberalism are widely shared in all modern political cultures—not just in comprehensive doctrines, liberal or other-wise, but in the hearts and minds of most (though, of course, not literally all) citizens. Political liberals claim that the overlapping consensus they would con-struct is more inclusive than any consensus built on a commitment to particular and potentially contentious values could be. They are right, of course; or rather they would be right if they could show that support for a liberal constitutional regime actually is implicit in the many comprehensive doctrines they would in-corporate into an overlapping consensus. But even if they could make good on this claim, it is far from clear why it would matter, if support for autonomy and self-realization is, in fact, as extensive as I claim.

Political liberals think it would matter for a reason that is, broadly speaking, contractarian. After its claims about de facto stability are sorted out and disen-tangled from its account of de jure political authority, political liberalism de-volves into a theory of political legitimacy based on consent. Its guiding idea is that political authority is justified if and only if the people who live under it consent to its rule. The requisite consent is *latent* in "reasonable" comprehen-sive doctrines. Thus, to secure de facto legitimacy, they urge that support for liberal constitutional arrangements be teased out of these comprehensive doc-trines wherever possible—the better to assure social stability. But insofar as the issue is de jure legitimacy, political liberals take over the principle that motivates all consent theories: individuals must somehow agree to be coerced before they can be coerced rightfully. Political liberalism's wrinkle on this old idea is that the requisite agreement is, in fact, implicit in the reasonable comprehensive doc-trines (most) citizens already endorse.

Unlike some traditional contractarian accounts of political legitimacy, political liberalism does not require unanimous consent. Not everyone needs to accept the right of the regime to use force, even if acceptance is understood in the very attenuated sense that political liberals propose. In the political liberal view, it is only a subset of the citizenry who must consent (implicitly) to the authority of the regime—those who subscribe to reasonable comprehensive doctrines. If in-deed there are as many or nearly as many proponents of the values instrumental liberals endorse as there are proponents of reasonable comprehensive doctrines, then political liberalism is no more inclusive or only marginally more inclusive than instrumental liberalism. But inclusion among those who would opt out of a "state of nature" is the consent theorist's way of according equal respect for moral personality. If political liberalism fares no better or only marginally better than instrumental liberalism in this respect, it cannot be deemed superior on the grounds that it is significantly more respectful of moral personality. This is why, even when de jure legitimacy is unambiguously the issue, the numbers count.

It could be objected that what matters is not the number of supporters a regime can command but the nature of their support. Thus a political liberal might say that what legitimates a liberal state is the reasonableness of the posi-tions that underwrite its liberal institutions, not the intuition's prevalence in the actual population. But it is unclear why reasonableness should have this legitimacy-conferring property, that is, why it should matter politically (rather than metaphysically). Kantian liberals defend liberal constitutional arrangements by appeal to the nature of practical reason. They maintain that liberal institutional arrangements are rationally prescribed. But unless political liberals are crypto-Kantians and therefore not political liberals at all, they can hardly appeal to reason itself. Thus it is reasonableness, not rationality, that political liberals invoke. But then it remains to explain what reasonableness has to do with legitimacy, and to do so in a way that is neither question-begging nor "metaphysical." Neither Rawls nor anyone else has yet done anything of the sort. I would venture that no one ever will: first because it is implausible on the face of it that an appropriately political explanation can be provided and, second, because, as we have seen, reasonableness is a vague and equivocal concept.

Reasonableness does not and almost certainly cannot do the requisite consent-conferring work. But the political liberal's recourse to reasonableness nevertheless profoundly affects the execution of the justificatory program political liberalism envisions. As remarked, the way contractarians would respect the moral equality of persons is by including everyone on equal terms in freely determined agreements. This is why traditional contractarian accounts of political authority require unanimity—for the state of nature to end, everyone must endorse the social contract. Political liberalism falls into this contractarian fold. But for political liberals, *unreasonableness* is a ground for excluding conceptions of the good from the requisite consensus. Thus, in the political liberal view, political institutions can rightfully command individuals who would not accept their authority even in principle.

In advancing this view, political liberalism effectively applies what was previously a standard move *within* liberal theory to its own justificatory program. *Unreasonableness* plays a role with respect to political legitimacy similar to the role that *incompetence* plays in traditional liberal understandings of tolerance. Under liberal institutions, the liberty of the incompetent (children, for example, and also individuals who are mentally or morally impaired) is not guaranteed; such persons can rightfully be treated paternalistically. Individuals who have not (or not yet) crossed the relevant competency thresholds and who are therefore not appropriate beneficiaries of tolerant treatment are, as it were, wards of the others. Analogously, individuals whose (imputed) comprehensive doctrines fail to meet the test of reasonableness (assuming that the idea can somehow be made sufficiently specific) can be rightfully carried along by the rest. They are not persons whose consent we need to take into account. Were most people incompetent, and therefore most appropriately treated as wards of the state, we could not expect to create a genuinely liberal society. Similarly, were most people's comprehensive doctrines unreasonable, we could not expect to implement respect for moral personality in the way that political liberalism supposes. It is therefore a question of luck, *political luck,* whether the liberal project generally and the political liberal project in particular can succeed. In the one case, what matters is that enough people are sufficiently competent to warrant the rights and immunities liberalism confers. In the other case, everything depends on whether most comprehensive doctrines do in fact imply support for liberal constitutional arrangements.

It is therefore fair to conclude that only the *extent* of an overlapping consensus could warrant the claim that political liberalism respects the moral equality of persons better than instrumental liberalism. Thus political liberalism's supposed superiority with respect to de jure legitimacy rests on the same contention as does its purported advantages for de facto legitimacy. This is one reason why the problems of de facto and de jure legitimacy are so closely intertwined in the political liberal literature. Whether political liberals acknowledge it or not, the advantages they claim for political liberalism depend on the way the world is: on the purported fact that some nonliberal comprehensive doctrines, the reasonable ones, implicitly underwrite support for liberal constitutional regimes; and on the claim that reasonable comprehensive doctrines have effectively crowded their unreasonable competitors out of the political arena. If it is in fact the case that support for the core valuational commitments of instrumental liberalism is nearly as widespread and as deep as adherence to reasonable comprehensive doctrines is, the purported superiority of political liberalism's purchase on both de facto and de jure legitimacy would effectively disappear.

Liberalism Forever?

The move from "metaphysical" to political liberalism may not matter in the ways that political liberals suppose. But the ascendancy of political liberalism does matter *politically*. Political liberalism is an obstacle in the way of ideal theories that transcend the horizons of ongoing social and political practices. Ironically, in view of its connections with liberal egalitarianism, political liberalism is *more conservative* from an egalitarian point of view, more supportive of existing (liberal) practices and institutional arrangements, than Mill's less obviously egalitarian theory is.

Instrumental liberalism suggests what political liberalism blocks. It suggests that neutrality is not an end in itself but a means for advancing values connected to an admittedly particular, but nevertheless uncontroversial, conception of the good for human beings. It suggests, in other words, the possibility of *other means* than neutrality for achieving these ends, for advancing autonomy and self-realization. It is, I maintain, for the sake of an ideal theory beyond liberal egalitarianism, a theory that follows the egalitarian idea to its ultimate destination, that the difference between political and instrumental liberalism matters.

There is plainly something right about Rawls's conviction that fundamental differences in comprehensive doctrines will never entirely disappear in modern pluralistic communities. There probably never will come a time when everyone will agree about everything that matters fundamentally. Thus the conditions that warrant neutrality are permanent. But can we obtain the benefits of neutrality without institutions of the sort that liberal societies have developed? I will argue in the following chapters that we can, at least to some degree. My point for now is just that instrumental liberalism is more hospitable to this idea than political liberalism.

Political liberalism presents itself as a philosophy for an indefinite future. It suggests nothing beyond liberal institutions themselves, implying that in the best of all possible worlds, liberal constitutionalism would remain indefinitely in place. Instrumental liberalism, on the other hand, suggests the possibility that yet more effective means to liberal ends can be contrived than the ones liberalism proffers—provided, of course, that the conditions that engendered liberal institutions and that continue to sustain them are suitably transformed. Unlike political liberalism, instrumental liberalism is open in principle to a political theory and practice beyond its own doctrinal commitments and practical recommendations. It is a philosophy that suggests its own eventual transcendence.

But it suggests this possibility only to those who seek it out. Like liberals generally, instrumental liberals typically blind themselves to the limits of liberalism. Here, again, Mill's example is illustrative. Mill defended tolerance on the grounds that it is an improver—it produces better outcomes (as measured by humanity's permanent and progressively unfolding interests) and also better individuals (capable of producing yet better outcomes in the future). It is plainly consistent with this position that, at some point, liberal institutions will have outlived their usefulness by becoming internalized in the dispositions of postliberal men and women. Mill did not draw this conclusion, however. As much as any political liberal, he envisioned liberal institutions continuing into an indefinite future. He did suggest, rather vaguely, that institutional arrangements would evolve as circumstances become increasingly fortuitous and as individuals' characters are transformed in ever more liberal ways. But he never seriously—or at least approvingly—contemplated a break with liberal practices and institutions themselves. The idea that liberalism can eventually transcend itself may be compatible with instrumental liberalism's theoretical commitments, but it is not, it seems, in line with the considered convictions of instrumental liberals.

Mill thought that as long as societies follow a generally liberal trajectory, institutional arrangements will evolve in the right way without fundamental ruptures. In contrast, socialists and other radicals have long maintained that deep transformations in political structures are indispensable conditions for progressive change. Thus, for Marx, once productive forces are sufficiently developed, capitalism is an impediment to human progress. Its overthrow and replacement by socialism and ultimately communism therefore becomes imperative. But because political "superstructures" ultimately accord with the functional requirements of the "economic base," the capitalist state is an obstacle in the way of capitalism's demise. To transform the base, it is therefore necessary to transform the superstructure too—in other words, to capture the capitalist state and then replace it with a form of political organization conducive to the political tasks at hand. In this respect, supraliberal egalitarians are closer to Marx than to Mill. But Millian instrumental liberalism at least raises the possibility of a fundamentally different political order.

Political liberals can entertain the thought (although they seldom do so) that it might be desirable to transform economic structures—perhaps for the sake of one or another distributional value. Thus Rawls himself has never repudiated the claim he made in *A Theory of Justice* that a socialist economic order can be just. But political liberals are committed in principle to the indefinite continuation of liberal political forms. The idea that it might someday be desirable to relax constitutional safeguards, the better to realize other ends, lies beyond the political liberal compass. In the short run, this failure of vision is benign. As we will see in Chapter 4, what egalitarians need now and for the foreseeable future is more liberalism, not less. In this sense, *any* conceptual undergirding of liberal institutional arrangements tends to direct humankind in a more egalitarian direction. But political liberalism impedes thinking about what lies beyond liberalism. I will go on to argue that it does so at a time when the development of a supraliberal democratic theory is crucial not just for moving humanity closer to what the best ideal theory recommends, but for quotidian politics as well. In contrast, instrumental liberalism puts liberalism itself in question, albeit by implication only. It ought therefore to be the egalitarian's justifying theory of choice, for, as we will see, the political liberal's principled agnosticism about all but the most uncontroversial fundamental values is an obstacle in the way of the fullest possible implementation of egalitarian aims. If egalitarians follow Rawls along the political liberal path, supraliberal egalitarianism may lie forever out of reach.

4

Beyond Liberal Democracy

Liberalism and democracy have been joined for more than a century and a half. But even years of peaceful coexistence cannot obliterate a long-standing tension between them. The problem, in short, is that democracy, the rule of the *demos,* appears to threaten the immunities from state interference that liberalism seeks to protect. Liberal democracy has therefore always been an uneasy combination. My aim in this chapter is to investigate the prospects for overcoming this state of affairs. To this end, I suggest the possibility of a *supra-liberal democracy,* a political theory and practice *beyond* liberal democracy. Thus this chapter, like the preceding one, focuses mainly on issues in political theory, not on equality per se. But for reasons that will emerge, to venture *beyond* liberal egalitarianism, this detour is indispensable. To transcend liberal equality, it is necessary to transcend liberal democracy too.

I begin with some observations on liberal democratic theory and practice, arguing that the dominant liberal democratic synthesis has been achieved mainly at democracy's expense. Then I contend that democracy, like liberalism, is best viewed instrumentally, at least in the historical conditions that now obtain and that are likely to obtain for the foreseeable future. In defense of these claims, I make extensive use of some ideas of Rousseau's, drawing particularly on those aspects of his political philosophy that support claims for the *transformative* effects of democratic institutions. Finally, I resume the discussion of liberalism begun in Chapter 3—with a view to joining liberal concerns to democratic institutional arrangements in ways that can be expected actually to advance democracy while still according liberal values their due.

To argue in favor of a transformative politics is, of course, to speculate about the likely consequences of yet unrealized institutional arrangements on the characters of individuals living under them. It is therefore in the nature of the case that nothing can be settled definitively by philosophical arguments alone or by appeal to the authority of Rousseau or any other historical figure, or even by reflecting on pertinent empirical evidence. There is scant experience of radical democracy even at levels below the state, and no experience at all of full-fledged political entities run in radically democratic ways. There is much more data bearing on how liberal institutions affect people's characters, but there is no uncontroversial way to ascertain the relevance of this evidence, and no way to interpret it unequivocally. The conclusions that follow therefore have a necessarily tentative cast.

Not long ago, many readers would have found the claims I will make in behalf of democracy obvious. But nowadays, pessimism about human nature and the human condition, a perennial theme of conservative thought, has become pervasive. Thus I expect that my account of democracy will strike many readers as hopelessly utopian. I would point out, however, that today's "realism" rests on considerations that are no more substantiated, philosophically or empirically, than those to which I appeal in defense of my more "utopian" stance. In short, there is no way, at present, to adjudicate this dispute conclusively. But even if an incontrovertible case in support of democracy's beneficial transformative effects cannot be made, a case at least as plausible as any supporting contrary views can. I attempt to mount such a case and thereby justify faith in the possibility of a world in which a far more radical and thoroughgoing democracy than liberal democratic theory proffers will finally come into its own. However, the barely democratic aspect of liberal democratic theory is not my only target. I take on the antiliberal biases of Rousseau and other radical democrats too. Thus I argue for the necessity of liberalism for the foreseeable future—not just for the reasons surveyed in Chapter 3 but also for the sake of liberalism's own transformative effects. I argue, in short, that, to advance egalitarian aims, a deep and far-reaching, transformative liberalism is an indispensable complement to the full-fledged democratization of public life.

In our own largely untransformed world, liberal democracy almost certainly is morally compelling—to the detriment of the fullest possible realization of egalitarian aims. My claim in this chapter is that this unhappy state of affairs is changeable and that egalitarians, including liberal egalitarians, are (or ought to be) committed, by the force of their own valuational commitments, to bringing the requisite changes about.

Liberal Democracy

Originally, "democracy" meant what the word says: rule by the *demos,* the popular masses. So conceived, democracy was more often a theoretical possibility for philosophers than a practical objective for political actors, and among philosophers it was almost universally despised. However by the middle of the seventeenth century, as the first of the great revolutionary upheavals of the modern period began to unfold in England, democratic aspirations erupted onto the political agenda. Still, many decades would pass before "democracy" elicited the widespread approval it enjoys today, and it was not until the middle of the twentieth century that it came to be almost universally esteemed, even as its meaning was widely and essentially contested.[1] Not surprisingly, liberalism, which developed around the same time, fared better at first, at least among economic and intellectual elites. The principal concern of the first liberals was, after all, the defense of property rights against the state—and not incidentally against the (potentially redistributive) demands of the *demos*. Thus the first liberals feared democracy, and the first democrats were understandably reluctant to embrace liberal concerns.

Today, "democracy" has many senses. Sometimes, though, the term is still used in ways that descend from its original meaning. Thus, in some theoretical contexts, "democracy" denotes rule by an undifferentiated citizenry, in other words, by the *demos* along with everybody else. In this usage, the role of the *demos* is, of course, obscured. Partly in consequence of this fact, democrats today, even when they understand "democracy" in a way that connects conceptually to the term's original meaning, are seldom, if ever, as partisan on behalf of the popular masses as their predecessors were. But, however attenuated the class content of "democracy" may have become, remnants of the old idea plainly do survive.

Liberalism too has evolved considerably since its inception. Thus the commitment to equality that motivates liberal egalitarianism is almost certainly at odds with the first liberals' concern to defend private property and its unfettered accumulation. I will not dwell on these changes here, nor on the vicissitudes of liberalism's latter-day cohabitation with democracy. It will suffice to observe that the emergence of relatively stable liberal democratic regimes by the middle of the nineteenth century was won largely at democracy's expense. Democracy remains a component of liberal democratic theory and practice; democratic impulses survive in the political culture of liberal democratic regimes. But democracy's role in liberal democracy is so attenuated that it is tempting, if not altogether fair, to draw the cynical conclusion that liberal democrats are democrats only to the extent that official support for "democracy" is necessary in a world in which the entry of the popular masses into the political arena has become an irreversible fact. In any event, it is a remarkable consequence of the

---

[1] An "essentially contested" concept is one that (virtually) all sides officially endorse, even as they advance widely disparate and sometimes even incompatible views of its meaning. Nowadays, "equality of opportunity" is another essentially contested idea.

influence liberal democratic theory has come to exercise that the tension between liberalism and democracy that was once so widely appreciated is nowadays seldom even acknowledged. Thus it has become almost commonplace in
the mainstream political culture for "democracy" to denote the so-called Western democracies and regimes that resemble them—political systems that are as-
suredly (though imperfectly) liberal but in which the *demos* hardly rules.

Perhaps the most telling indication of the fact that liberal democracy reconciles liberalism and democracy at democracy's expense is the manifest hostility
of liberal democrats to the very idea of *direct* democracy. In its strongest version, direct democrats maintain that citizens are subject only to laws enacted by
the whole people. Thus Rousseau (1762) famously argued that representative
government, the alternative to direct democracy, actually usurps popular sovereignty. But Rousseau's position was never the norm. Most proponents of direct democracy did consider representative government permissible. It was
permissible because it was usually unavoidable—an unfortunate accommoda-
tion to the practical impossibility of assembling everyone together for public
deliberation and collective choice.[2] However, in the course of time, representative government has come to be seen, largely for liberal reasons, as preferable
to direct democracy—even in theory. Thus it is claimed that representatives are
more competent than the citizenry at large, less susceptible to despotic manip-
ulation, and above all more dedicated to advancing liberal concerns. For liberal
democrats today, it therefore suffices for the citizenry periodically to elect representatives to rule in their behalf, provided only that representatives are accountable to their respective constituencies. But even accountability is understood in a highly attenuated way. It is enough, it seems, if there is competition
for political office. The fact that the competitors may be of virtually one mind
on nearly all issues or that the voters may be obliged to select from among
what they perceive to be greater or lesser evils is seldom, if ever, taken to im-
pugn a regime's democratic character.[3] Thus liberalism has been joined to

---

[2]A different view of the institutional arrangements proposed in the *Federalist Papers* and established by the U.S. Constitution is urged by Bruce Ackerman (1988). In Ackerman's view, representative government (of the American sort) provides means for institutionalizing the popular will in
times of "normal" politics, when citizens are disinclined to assert themselves collectively but prefer
instead to consolidate the benefits of previous collective assertions, and also in more "revolutionary" moments, as in the period of constitutional change following the U.S. Civil War and to a lesser
extent during the New Deal. This is not the place to take on Ackerman's contentions except to note
the wistful character of its celebration of American institutions. Surely, the political system in place
in the United States—with its "imperial presidency," its winner-take-all and first-past-the-post voting systems, its vulnerability to influence peddling, and its manifest subordination to business interests—is remarkably unresponsive to anything that might be called a popular will, even in com-
parison to the institutional arrangements of other Western democracies.

[3] This situation is more acute in the United States than elsewhere, but it is becoming increasingly
the norm everywhere that liberal democratic regimes are firmly entrenched. But even where, as a
matter of fact, a (comparatively) wide range of views actually is represented within the mainstream

democracy by denuding democracy of its content. Unlike rule by the *demos* or even by an undifferentiated citizenry, in practice and sometimes in theory too, "democracy" designates nothing more than a political system in which those who govern—or rather a small subset of them, since most of the work of governance is performed by a more or less permanent bureaucracy—are chosen in competitive elections.

Earlier liberals and democrats, unlike (most) liberal democrats today, were acutely aware of the tension between liberalism and democracy and did attempt to make sense of it. But to understand how liberalism and democracy are at odds, it will not do to turn back the clock a century and a half, since the old consensus, reduced to its core, held that the conflict between liberalism and democracy is only a special case of the larger problem of reconciling democracy with "constitutionalism."[4] This view has merit, but it can also be misleading for democrats intent on forging a supraliberal democratic theory and practice.

The long recognized problem of constitutional democracy can be briefly put. Democracy implies popular control implemented through majority rule voting or some closely related collective choice rule. But constitutional measures restrict popular control. They mark off an area of law that is resistant to and, at the limit, immune from state-mandated changes, including changes determined through democratic procedures. "Constitutional democracy" might therefore seem an oxymoron. But, of course, constitutional arrangements are indispensable for democratic collective choice—if only in the sense that the collective choice rule itself is a constitutional provision. Thus it is clear that constitutionalism and democracy are not entirely incompatible. I would venture, in fact, that what at first appears to be a contradiction is actually a paradox, an apparent contradiction that points to a deeper truth—a deeper connection between democratic collective choice and constitutional constraints. That truth is just that constitutional constraints, even when they restrict the scope of democratic collective choice, can further democratic objectives in roughly the way that restrictions placed on agents' options can enhance their capacities for executing particular tasks or realizing particular objectives.[5] The idea in both cases is the same: by making ourselves unfree to do some of the things we may want to do

---

political culture, it is still the fact of political competition, not the liveliness of political debate, that is thought to render the political system democratic.

[4] The *locus classicus* for discussion of many of the problems raised by the conflict between constitutionalism and democracy is, of course, *The Federalist Papers*. For important contemporary reflections on these issues, see Elster and Slagstad 1988.

[5] Paradigmatic of this phenomenon is Ulysses, bound to the mast of his vessel so that he will be unfree to steer his vessel in the direction of the sirens' song and therefore able to do what he ultimately wants—to return to his home. This phenomenon is studied extensively in Elster 1979. For some constitutionalist applications, see Holmes 1995.

in the short run, we can sometimes enhance our ability to do the things we want to do in the long run. This lesson was already implicit in contractarian accounts of sovereignty. In contriving a sovereign, individuals restrict the freedom they enjoy in a state of nature. But in doing so, they advance their interests as free beings. Similarly, in enacting constitutional constraints on popular majorities, citizens may actually render themselves better able to implement their collective will—both because they protect their long-term interests from derailment by myopic popular majorities and because, by restricting the scope of collective choice, they are better able to concentrate their energies and therefore better able to legislate efficiently. Of course, it is not possible to conclude anything directly about *liberal* constraints on democratic collective choice from these very abstract considerations. To investigate the tension between democracy and liberalism and the possibility for its supersession, it will therefore be best to set aside the ostensible conflicts between democracy and constitutionalism in general and focus, more narrowly, on democracy and liberalism themselves.

Democracy: Is It an End or a Means?

Democracy can be defended on the grounds that it is instrumental for advancing some intrinsically desirable end or ends. Or it might be viewed as an end in itself or even promoted as a requirement of justice and therefore a necessary condition for normatively acceptable political arrangements. I would venture that most philosophical defenders of democracy believe that democracy is somehow an end in itself. But I think they are wrong. This side of communism, democracy is best viewed instrumentally (see Chapter 5).

Consider direct democracy first. As remarked, direct democracy is usually construed procedurally: political arrangements are democratic to the extent that social choices are determined (or at least consented to) collectively, where collective decisions are functions of individuals' choices among alternative outcomes in contention. A stronger but still procedural understanding of democracy would also include the requirement that the franchise be universal or nearly so, and a stronger conception still would mandate (some) rational deliberation and public debate. Why should adherence to democratic procedures, however construed, be regarded as an intrinsic good?

The question appears rhetorical. How, after all, could the way decisions are made matter for its own sake? Surely it cannot. I would submit that this impression is sound. But, on careful consideration, it is not at all obvious that it is—a point that becomes unavoidable when we realize that democrats and egalitarians appear to be in a similar situation. We could also ask why anyone should want a particular distributional pattern, one in which everyone has equivalent shares of the right distribuand, for its own sake? We know, however, that egalitarianism, liberal or otherwise, is hardly reducible to an expression of a preference for one kind of distribution, an equal one, over others, and we also know that equality is not a strictly instrumental value. This is not to deny that instrumental justifications for equal distributions are available.[6] But egalitarians accord equality pride of place mainly for noninstrumental reasons. Their claim is that the equal distribution of the right distribuand—or, if they are liberal egalitarians, equal distributions perturbed by individuals' free choices—implement a deeper notion of equal treatment, one which directly expresses the idea that, with respect to what matters fundamentally, everyone ought to count the same. In this sense, egalitarians value equality intrinsically; they consider it a requirement of justice. What egalitarians, liberal or otherwise, ultimately want is equal respect for moral personality or, as I shall sometimes say, *deep equality*. They are interested in equal distributions, subject perhaps to certain qualifications, because they believe that distributions of the right sort *implement* this ideal. I will argue later that this view is appropriate only under particular, though very long-standing, historical conditions. But in the world as it now is and as it is bound to remain for some time to come, equal distribution of the right distribuand does implement deep equality. To defend democratic collective choice procedures noninstrumentally, one would have to view them similarly. One would have to maintain that democracy is indispensable for implementing deep equality.

Can democratic collective choice be justified in this way? Although I give in the next chapter what could be construed as an affirmative answer, it would be misleading at this juncture to say yes. As I explain in Chapter 5, only in historical circumstances that have never in fact existed (but can come into being) will the equal distribution of democratic rights over all aspects of collective life finally *realize* what egalitarians ultimately want. In this chapter the issue is not what equality will require at the successful culmination of the egalitarian project, but how egalitarians ought to view democracy here and now. In the historical conditions that actually obtain, does it make sense to view democracy as an intrinsic good in the way that it makes sense, in these same conditions, to value equal distributions of the right distribuand?

It might appear so, for it would seem that when we make social choices functions of individuals' choices, each individual counting equally, we are according moral personality equal respect in the political sphere. Democracy would then be the analogue in politics of equality in the economy. But the parallel with egalitarian distribution is misleading. Equal distribution of the right distribuand *implements* deep equality; it puts equal treatment into practice. In con-

---

[6] For a classic statement of what equality is good for, see Shaw 1928. John Baker (1987) also suggests a number of respects in which equality is instrumentally valuable. Samuel Bowles and Herbert Gintis (1998) argue for equality in the same spirit when they maintain that a more equal distribution of (privately owned) productive assets can be efficiency enhancing. Cf. Levine 1998.

trast, equal participation in law making is not necessary for according persons equal respect; indeed, it can even be detrimental to that end, as I will presently suggest. Democratic decision procedures generally do advance deep equality. But they do so *contingently*. In this respect, democracy does not implement deep equality, even when it is instrumental for its realization.

The distinction between implementing a value and being instrumental for it may seem strained. But the difference is genuine and important. Equal distribution of the right distribuand is what makes the idea of deep equality concrete in historical conditions in which distributional questions are morally urgent. It is what deep equality *means* in these circumstances. On the other hand, the connection between democracy and deep equality is strictly causal. This is why the possibility that paternalistic governance may be more efficacious than democratic collective choice for advancing egalitarian objectives cannot be dismissed a priori. It is even conceivable that democratic procedures might actually be detrimental to deep equality in some circumstances, for example, when popular majorities pass measures that oppose the equal distribution of the right distribuand or when they diminish the political influence of minority groups. In sum, for an egalitarian, what matters is how people are treated by basic social institutions. Taking collective charge of one's own governance is nearly always preferable to paternalistic rule—not just because democratic participation can have beneficial transformative effects, but also for the familiar welfarist reasons adduced by Mill and others—that individuals generally know what will further their interests better than states do and that democratic procedures register this information better than alternative procedures.[7] But however formidable these considerations may be, the fact remains that there are no deeper, logical connections between equal participation in collective decision making and advancing equal respect for persons.

This consideration applies to direct democracy and is therefore relevant to liberal democratic theory to the extent that liberal democrats are proponents of direct democracy—in other words, to the extent that they would have citizens make collective choices directly, were it not impracticable. But as I have already pointed out, liberal democrats would not organize states along direct democratic lines even if they could. Partly to protect liberal values from the "tyranny of the majority," partly for the sake of social stability, and partly because they think it makes outcomes better, liberal democrats defend representative institutions,

[7] Nondemocratic decision procedures deny individuals the opportunity to register their views about what their own interests are. In contrast, democratic decision procedures generate outcomes by combining individuals' choices for alternatives in contention, where these choices typically represent individuals' interests (as the individuals themselves conceive them) and where all individuals' votes count equally. Where supermajorities are required to make enactments, the decision procedure is effectively weighted in favor of the status quo (because minorities are able to block positive enactments). Simple majority rule voting is therefore maximally efficacious for representing individuals' judgments about their own best interests. For further elaboration, see Levine 1976, 60–63.

not as second-best approximations of an unrealizable direct democratic ideal but as an ideal in its own right. Thus even if direct democrats can somehow construe democracy as an end in itself, it still would not follow that liberal democrats can; for in representative democracies, citizens do not make the decisions that affect their lives. Citizens only periodically elect the persons who make these decisions for them, or, more precisely, select such persons from a set of choices over which they have very little control. To this extent, they hold their representatives accountable for representing their interests. But as Rousseau might have said, it is one thing to select one's master and something else to be the master of oneself. It is clearly implausible to claim that a political system that eschews equal participation in collective decision making on principled grounds implements equal respect for persons through its reliance on democratic procedures. The connection is far too attenuated.

I will offer some suggestions presently about what democracy might be instrumental for. Before doing so, however, it will be instructive to eliminate one historically important kind of instrumentalist justification that instrumental liberals, influenced by Mill, might be tempted to adduce in democracy's behalf—the idea that democracy can be defended on utilitarian grounds.

There is, of course, no reason to hold that democracy is likely to make things worse, in any of the senses of "worse" that utilitarians acknowledge—no reason to think that democracy diminishes overall happiness or that it leaves individuals' desires less satisfied than they might be under alternative political arrangements. But there is also no reason to conclude the contrary. Benevolent despotism is the political expression of paternalism, the specter that Mill sought to banish from his defense of liberty. But even allowing, as Mill insisted, that individuals are generally better judges of their own interests than any state can be, and taking the preference sensitivity advantages of majority rule voting into account,[8] there is still no reason to conclude that aggregating individuals' choices democratically will reliably produce more utility than the judgments of wise benevolent despots. Majorities can fail to discover what will in fact maximize utility. What a Millian can say with confidence about genuinely democratic voting procedures is that they combine individuals' choices *fairly*—in other words, that the outcomes of votes reflect the relative strengths of different positions within the voting community.[9] There may be good reasons to vest confidence in an aggregating mechanism that has this property. But there is no reason to think that, in doing so, overall (or average) utility will be maximized.

---

[8] See note 7.

[9] Strictly speaking, this claim can only be made for direct democracies in which, in practice as well as in theory, voters are equally able to influence electoral outcomes. Needless to say, no liberal democracy meets this standard even approximately.

To hold otherwise would be to ascribe a property to democratic collective choice even stronger than the property that Adam Smith famously imputed to (idealized) market transactions. What Smith (1937) maintained is that in genuinely free markets, when individuals seek to do what is best for themselves individually, they will produce outcomes that are socially best, as if through the workings of an "invisible hand." Nearly two centuries after Smith made this conjecture, neoclassical economists have established a rather attenuated version of Smith's claim (see Debreu 1959). Thus it is demonstrable that in genuinely free markets—that is, in markets in which individuals are, among other things, perfectly informed about the consequences of their choices, and in which there are no economies of scale, no transaction costs, no externalities, and no monopolies—socially optimal outcomes do emerge whenever individuals seek to bring about the best outcomes for themselves, subject to the technological and budgetary constraints they confront. But "optimality" in this context has a precise, nonutilitarian sense. It means *Pareto optimality*. A state of affairs is Pareto optimal if any alteration would make someone worse off, where "worse off" is understood in a welfarist way. Thus Smith's contention, refracted through the prism of neoclassical economic analysis, amounts to this: If we take individuals' preferences, the distribution of resources among individuals, and production technologies across the economy as given, and if we assume that individuals are rational utility maximizers, the allocation of resources at the societal level will be Pareto optimal at equilibrium; that is, after all markets clear, any change in the allocation of resources would diminish at least one person's welfare. Pareto optimality is a welfarist standard. But it is weaker than the welfarist standard utilitarians invoke, the utility maximum. Thus there are infinitely many Pareto optimal allocations. All of them, along with those that are not Pareto optimal, yield distinct utility levels. Utilitarians would have society implement the one that produces the most utility or, in case of ties, to select from among the maximal set. Plainly, this is an exceedingly demanding requirement. There is no reason to expect that democratic voting will produce anything like it.

Benevolent despotism is a form of paternalism, focused on collectivities rather than individuals. But this difference changes nothing. For a utilitarian to defeat paternalism with respect to some category of proposed state intervention, it would be necessary, following Mill's example, to reflect on the likely consequences of paternalistic interventions or their absence in particular instances. Thus in defending free speech, Mill claimed that in the conditions that obtain in "civilized" societies, the consequences of free expression are almost always preferable, in a utilitarian sense, to any form of state interference with speech. In defense of this contention, he offered empirical speculations based partly on reflections on the detrimental consequences of past experiences of intolerance (Mill 1956, chap. 2). He did not argue on a priori grounds that paternalistic interventions are bound to make outcomes worse. Similarly plausible empirical speculations and historical ruminations directed against benevolent despotism would have to be made by anyone attempting to defend democratic collective choice in the same way. There is no reason to expect that satisfactory arguments of this kind will be forthcoming, and, in their absence, there is no reason to conclude that it is better for enhancing happiness or desire-satisfaction, to leave individuals to their own devices. In short, there is no basis for justifying democratic decision procedures on utilitarian grounds.

Instrumental Democracy

For defending democracy instrumentally, Rousseau's (1762) account of the moral foundation of the state is a useful starting point. Rousseau was perhaps the first philosopher to identify democracy with a particular decision procedure, majority rule voting. But democracy, for Rousseau, has little to do with what political philosophers nowadays call "proceduralism." Proceduralists view voters' choices as exogenous variables, as givens. How voters form choices therefore falls outside the scope of normative political philosophy in much the way that the formation of consumers' choices falls outside the scope of standard economic analyses of consumer behavior. Any view of democracy that prescribes deliberation or in any other way takes the formation of voters' choices into account would therefore be non- or extra-proceduralist. For Rousseau, no interesting or even plausible view of democracy could be proceduralist because, in his view, how choices are formed matters decisively. At the very least, choices must be informed by rational deliberation and public debate. This is why, in characterizing democratic collective choice, I have depicted deliberation and debate, along with voting, as "procedures." I have, in other words, adopted Rousseau's understanding, not the proceduralists'.

In this respect, Rousseau's position is easily assimilable to mainstream, liberal democratic views (see, for example, Barber 1984). Otherwise, however, Rousseau's *differences* from contemporary ways of thinking about democracy are so far-reaching that the pertinence of his ideas can be difficult to grasp. The issue, ultimately, is not whether voters' choices are given or mutable. Obviously, they are mutable, even if some democratic theorists consider this fact irrelevant to normative political philosophy. The question, for Rousseau, is what voters' choices represent: whether they register what Rousseau calls "private interests" or whether, instead, they represent judgments about the "general will." The mainstream understanding, according to which voting combines voters' preferences, instantiates the former idea. Rousseau adamantly opposed this model of voting.

Rousseau's underlying contention was that rightful political authority exists only if each individual "obeys only himself" (1762, bk. 1, chap. 6). He then maintained that for this condition to hold, individuals must join together into a single community, united by a strong (notional) consensus on ends. Citizens must want the same thing, the general interest, even as they may be differently cognizant of what the general interest is. When the requisite consensus exists, individuals are moved by a single "motive force," the general will.[10] Thus when citizens vote as members of "the moral and collective body" that they freely constitute through the social contract, they do not express their preferences for alternative outcomes in contention, as mainstream liberal democratic theorists suppose. Rather, they express their opinion about what the general will is or, in other words, about what their own interests are insofar as they are integral members of the collective entity they comprise. This is why the method of majority rule is not a preference-aggregating mechanism in Rousseau's political philosophy but a truth-discovery procedure. By voting, citizens *discover* what the general will is. Individuals who are on the losing side of some vote are therefore mistaken about what their interests qua citizens are. Thus, when the majority rules, even voters who are in the minority "obey only themselves." If the state compels them, it is only to do what they really want to do, whether they know it or not. As Rousseau maintained, the state "forces . . . [its citizens] to be free." Far from being at odds, then, authority and autonomy are reconciled — indeed, identified — in systems of direct, majoritarian rule.

For Rousseau, the end that democracy serves is obedience to a law of one's own making, "autonomy." Thus it serves the same end that liberalism serves for Mill and other instrumental liberals. But Rousseau's highly idiosyncratic and deeply suggestive account is more complex than the instrumental liberal's. In the Rousseauian scheme, democracy is instrumental for autonomy in at least two ways. In just states, where individuals qua citizens are "under the supreme direction of the general will," it is the mechanism through which the general will is discovered. But in a more immediately political sense, because democratic *participation* is transformative, democratic procedures are one of several means through which the education of individuals' characters toward full democratic citizenship is achieved. Democratic participation is the objective of political association, but it is also a means through which legitimate political association becomes possible. It is a condition for its own possibility.

These positions converge on a very particular and largely implicit understanding of *community,* an idea marked by a revealing ambiguity. On the one hand, the argument of *The Social Contract* is deeply communitarian. For authority and autonomy to be reconciled, the radically independent individuals who populate the state of nature must join together to form a collective entity moved by a single will. Moreover, to implement this ideal politically, all the institutions of society must work together to assure the subordination of private wills to the general will. Thus the imperative that guides Rousseauian politics is

---

[10] I defend the cogency of this idea in Levine 1976, 1993.

to foster a sense of community and, in doing so, to transform atomic individuals into citizens.[11] In this respect, Rousseau is a *republican,* albeit an unconventional one, an exemplar of that tradition in political philosophy that accords pride of place to civic virtue and that depicts the existence of strong communal feelings as a prerequisite for legitimate political arrangements. It is also fair to say, however that Rousseau is not interested at all in community for its own sake; he prizes community only for its efficacy in promoting autonomy. Rousseau's communitarianism, however central it may be to his vision of the just state, remains only instrumental.

Even so, there is a good Rousseauian reason for regarding community as an end in itself, suggested by the spirit, if not the letter, of *The Social Contract.* The idea accords with an understanding of freedom that Rousseau, like other republican writers, cherished, an idea that differs from autonomy but coexists with it and bears a conceptual affinity to it.[12] What I have in mind is the ancient understanding of freedom as a juridical status: of the *free* man or woman in contrast to the slave or, more relevantly, the *free* city or state in contrast to subordinated political communities. A city or state is free if it is independent and self-governing. This sense of freedom and the idea of community that Rousseau's vision of ideal political arrangements suggests are interconnected. The republican ideal of civic virtue, according to which citizens place the interests of their respective communities above their own private interests, reinforces and strengthens the political independence of the state. At the same time, political independence is a condition for the fullest possible manifestation of civic virtue; only free states can be genuine (political) communities. The republicans who articulated these intuitions were less inclined or less able than Rousseau to elaborate their views theoretically. There is therefore no single term in the literature that quite captures their ideal. But *republican community* serves the purpose. Neither Rousseau nor any other republican writer expressly developed a notion of republican community as an end in itself. However, *The Social Contract* does suggest an instrumentalist rationale for democracy that appeals to this idea. If only implicitly, it advances the idea that rule by an undifferentiated citizenry, free from external domination, is necessary for republican community and also instrumental for its enhancement. In other words, it proposes that republican community too is a condition for its own possibility.

This instrumentalist defense of democracy accords more with the political than the philosophical aspect of Rousseau's thought. In the opening chapters of *The Social Contract,* the state is a regulative idea, the Platonic form of legitimate political order. It is at this level of abstraction from actual political arrangements that the method of majority rule is construed as a procedure for discov-

---

[11] I elaborate on these claims and those that follow in Levine 1976, 159–86; 1987, 39–49.

[12] A case for the timeliness of this strain of political philosophy is set forth in Pettit 1997.

ering the general will and justified by the "rectitude" of the outcomes it produces. From a somewhat less abstract vantage point, the regulative idea becomes a political objective, a goal to be attained or, so far as possible, approximated in real-world conditions. In this sense, republican community is
something to strive toward. Thus the social contract establishes the just state
notionally and, at the same time, inaugurates the (potentially protracted)
process of its construction. But since the state that Rousseau envisioned comprises just individuals—themselves under that "form of association" that renders them integral parts of the whole by joining them together under "the
supreme direction of the general will"—the struggle for community is effectively a struggle for the will of each individual. It is a struggle for what
eighteenth-century writers called "opinion." What is at stake is the character of
these individuals, their dispositions to subordinate private to general interests.
The *process* of democratic deliberation and collective choice, much more than
the outcome of votes, is crucial in this endeavor. Paradoxically, therefore, the
"rectitude" of the decisions voters render is less important than their participation in electoral procedures—including, of course, the public deliberations that
are prerequisite for democratic collective choice. The end matters less than the
means. From a political point of view, republican community is not so much a
condition for political legitimacy as it is its objective. It is an intrinsic good for
which democracy is instrumental.

It was this aspect of Rousseau's thought that Marx seized upon and developed,
wittingly or not, in developing his vision of communism (small *c*), the unifying
principle and ultimate objective of *Marxist* political practice.[13] The relevance of
this idea for equality will be a theme of Chapter 5. What I would note here is how
communism (small *c*)—or, more precisely, the normative commitments that un-
derlie it—suggest yet another end for which democracy is instrumental.

Marx was famously reluctant to elaborate upon his vision of a communist future, but the few celebrated descriptions he did advance—for example, the as-
sertion in *The Communist Manifesto* that under communism "the free development of each . . . [will be] the condition for the free development of all"[14]—
indicate a commitment not only to autonomy, but also to a particular view of
excellence, attained through the *development* of individuals' capacities under ideal
conditions (or rather ideal conditions relativized to historical circumstances). It
therefore follows that political arrangements are justified, in part, to the extent
that they enhance individual self-realization, the development of inborn powers. Among these essentially human capacities are those that are indispensable

[13] This claim is developed extensively in Levine 1987, 1993. When I spell "communism" with a
small *c*, the intent is to distinguish Marx's objective from Communism, the social, political, and
economic regime installed in the former Soviet Union and elsewhere.
[14] Marx and Engels 1962, 1:54.

to (active) citizenship: the ability to deliberate to good effect, both individually and collectively, and an inclination to join with one's fellow citizens in collective endeavors for common ends. Thus political participation in democratic institutions is indispensable for full self-realization. As Aristotle proclaimed, human beings are "political animals." In this respect, Aristotle and Marx are of one mind.[15]

Again, there is no expression in common use that captures this idea exactly, but *Aristotelian self-realization* will serve the purpose. My claim, then, is that one end for which democracy is instrumental is republican community, and another is Aristotelian self-realization. These objectives are conceptually distinct but causally connected. Democratic collective choice is instrumental for Aristotelian self-realization not only because it recommends a high level of popular participation in political processes but also for its educative effects. The transformation of individuals into republican citizens also involves the unfolding of individuals' capacities, including their political capacities, in the way partisans of Aristotelian self-realization envision. If human beings truly are political animals, in becoming democratic citizens they develop or realize what they intrinsically are. They self-realize.

Following Aristotle's lead, we may regard human self-realization as a freestanding and multifaceted objective. It includes the development of political capacities, but much else too. Democracy probably has little effect on many aspects of self-realization. It is therefore not instrumental for self-realization generally. But it *is* indispensable for realizing at least some capacities essential to living a fully human life. We have seen how a similar idea informs instrumental liberalism.

In sum, then, democracy does admit of instrumentalist justifications. Rousseauian and Marxian political philosophies suggest at least three relatively independent instrumentalist rationales. The first, which is the most clearly Rousseauian in provenance and therefore also the most idiosyncratic and controversial, maintains that democracy is instrumental for freedom or, more specifically, for autonomy, "obedience to a law one has legislated oneself." The second, which is Rousseauian in spirit, holds that democracy is instrumental for fostering republican community. The third, which draws on aspects of Marx's political theory and therefore on Rousseau only indirectly, harkens back to Aristotelian themes, defending democracy for its effects on self-realization. The availability of these rationales and the evident plausibility of at least the latter two counter the temptation to regard democratic collective choice as an end in itself. There may be no satisfactory utilitarian justification for democracy, but democracy can be defended instrumentally nevertheless.

---

[15] Connections between Aristotle and Marx are examined in Gilbert 1990, chap. 7.

Toward a New Fusion

I argued in Chapter 3 that instrumental liberalism is more conducive to efforts at transcending liberal horizons through the radical democratization of the public realm than political liberalism is. The preceding discussion of instrumental democracy suggests another reason why. Instrumental liberalism and radical democracy advance roughly the same ends. They are therefore susceptible to being made to work in concert. This possibility points the way toward a new fusion of liberal and democratic concerns, one not achieved at democracy's expense.

To the detriment of egalitarian aims, liberal democracy addresses the long-standing tension between liberalism and democracy by minimizing democracy. It is crucial that democrats not do the opposite—at least not before the need for liberal protections withers away. Until such a time is reached, if it ever is, it would be disastrous to minimize liberalism, even for the sake of the values for which democracy is instrumental. It is fair to say that recent history has made this exigency evident. The historical experience of Communism (big C) shows that liberal constraints on public authorities are crucial for protecting individuals from a tyranny more detrimental to the values shared by democrats, liberals, and communists (small c) too than liberal democracy's mitigation of its democratic component. There can be little doubt therefore that under existing conditions the consequences of tampering with liberal safeguards would be dangerously reckless. Supraliberal democrats should resist this temptation by all means.

The first liberals inveighed against the tyranny of the majority. Their principal concern, however, was not that individuals' conceptions of the good be treated fairly or, more generally, that individuals be accorded equal respect. Their aim was to secure rights to hold and accumulate property without state interference. It became clear long ago that liberal democracy poses no threat in this regard. Its institutional arrangements effectively nullify any challenge the *demos* might pose to propertied interests. But the early liberals' intuitions were sound: genuine democracy *is* a threat to private property. The problem is not quite the tyranny of the majority. A democratic citizenry is unlikely to organize plunder under the cover of law. The threat to property comes from the fact, already intimated (in Chapter 2) and soon to be defended (in Chapter 5), that a radical transformation of property rights is a prerequisite for real democracy—for governance of, by, and for the people.

As remarked, philosophers usually think of liberalism *constitutionally,* as a system of rules proscribing particular types of state or societal interferences with individuals' lives and behaviors. A state is liberal if it is neutral with respect to competing conceptions of the good or, what comes to the same thing, if it (actively) tolerates speech and other expressions of private conscience, diversity, and experiments in living. It is plainly useful for many purposes to depict liberalism this way. But just as construing liberalism constitutionally threatens to obscure what is central to liberal *politics,* doing so also obscures the way toward resolving liberalism's tensions with democracy. We ought therefore, once again, to recall that liberalism's distinctive constitutional arrangements require individuals of the right sort, liberal citizens. Constitutional measures enforcing tolerance will work effectively only if individuals are disposed to be tolerant in their absence; and the more liberal its citizens are, the more flourishing a liberal regime will be. Just as democracy is about transforming individuals into democrats, liberalism is about making people liberal.

Liberals need liberal constraints on state power to countervail dispositions on the part of voters that would otherwise result in illiberal collective choices. But the more liberal the citizens become, the less needful such correctives are. The more liberalism succeeds, the more the long-standing tension between liberalism and democracy will be mitigated. Thus liberalism can transform the conditions that make liberal safeguards necessary, rendering itself increasingly superfluous. In this sense, liberal constitutionalism aims at its own demise.

This position too was anticipated by Rousseau.[16] The authority of the state founded by the social contract is absolute in principle. There is nothing that a Rousseauian sovereign, the people themselves under a "form of association" in which each individual "places himself under the supreme direction of the general will," cannot rightfully do. But, in a well-functioning state, the sovereign will not in fact intrude extensively into the lives and behaviors of its subjects. The sovereign will limit itself without constitutional proscription, because "nothing happens without a cause" sufficient for explaining its effects, and illiberal violations of individuals' rights will seldom, if ever, have a sufficient reason in a healthy polity. In principle, the sovereign may do anything; in practice, the sovereign will likely do nothing to which liberals might object.

In the end, however, it is impossible to attribute to Rousseau a clear and unambiguous account of the connection between democratic institutions and liberal values in a just state. He was too unsystematic a thinker. Even his commitment to participatory democracy was equivocal.[17] But participatory democrats influenced by Rousseau and intent on enlisting his authority in support of their views can plausibly argue that, for him, radical democratization suffices to protect liberal values. Rousseau certainly evinced no confidence in liberal institutions themselves. But whatever Rousseau might have thought or participatory democrats may still believe, liberalism complements radical democratization. As mainstream liberalism has evolved from a justificatory theory of market capitalism to a philosophy of tolerance, it has become apparent that liberalism and

---

[16] See Rousseau 1762, bk. 2, chaps. 4–5. I discuss these chapters of *The Social Contract* in Levine 1976, 72–79, where I elaborate upon the claims advanced in this paragraph.

[17] For conflicting interpretations, see Pateman 1970, chap. 2; Fralin 1978.

democracy serve the same masters. They are instrumental for the same ends, though differentially efficacious, depending, in part, on the historical contexts in which they are deployed. Thus liberalism and democracy need not be at odds. In the right conditions, they can operate in tandem to advance their common aims.

The existence of a real consensus on ends, deeper and not much narrower than the overlapping consensus upon which political liberals stake their hopes for both de facto and de jure legitimacy, provides a basis for a political theory *beyond* liberal democracy. Insofar as political liberals are dedicated to *conserving* liberal institutions, they have reason to fear this departure from the justificatory strategy they favor. Supraliberal democracy does challenge existing institutional arrangements, specifically those that diminish democratic governance. There is a sense therefore in which supraliberal democracy puts the bases of social and political stability in jeopardy; it threatens the de facto legitimacy of liberal democratic regimes. But liberal democracy can only go so far toward realizing the values liberals and democrats share. In the end, it blocks the emergence of that "moral and collective body" Rousseau envisioned, a condition that is indispensable, finally, for the fulfillment of liberal and democratic—and therefore, implicitly, liberal democratic—aims. In this sense, it blocks a deeper social unity than political liberalism is equipped to comprehend.

Autonomy, republican community and Aristotelian self-realization are values one could reasonably reject, especially if "reasonableness" is construed in the expansive, political liberal way. But even political liberals can take consolation from the fact that a supraliberal democratic regime would never seek to further these values directly. Because supraliberals remain resolutely liberal for as long as need be, they endeavor to advance their ends indirectly—in consequence of the workings of liberal and democratic institutions. It could hardly be otherwise. The advancement of the values liberalism and democracy share probably cannot come about through deliberately undertaken programs. In all likelihood, the desired result can only be a by-product of the liberalization and democratization of the regime.[18] In sum, it is neutrality itself—in conjunction with extensive popular participation in democratic deliberative and legislative bodies—that does the transformative work that is prerequisite for *superseding* liberal democracy.

Supraliberal democracy is not antiliberal in the way that liberal democracy is implicitly antidemocratic. It does not aim at liberalism's suppression or mitigation but at its "supersession." Supraliberal democracy would "realize" liberalism by transforming citizens into liberals. Thus it would have liberal institutions— but not liberal protections—*wither away* in order that democracy might finally come into its own. Its goal, in short, is nothing less than a political order that,

---

[18] On states that are "essentially by-products," see Elster 1983, chap. 2.

unlike liberal democracy, fulfills both liberal and democratic aspirations whole-heartedly and unequivocally.

It is not only because there will likely always be recalcitrant individuals that it is dangerous to suppose that liberal constitutional protections can rapidly become superfluous. There is also the fact that the constitution itself is an educator, a constant and public reminder of the rules that constitute the political community as it develops in the direction of its deepest valuational commitments. But insofar as the aim is to fuse liberalism and democracy without diminishing one or the other, it is misleading to *identify* liberalism with its constitutional proscriptions; for what is required, in the end, is not quite that laws forbid states from intruding into aspects of individuals' lives and behaviors, but that human beings be transformed in such a way and to such an extent that in a radically democratized social order such intrusions would seldom, if ever, occur. A liberal constitution is instrumental in this regard; indeed, in anything like the conditions that now obtain, it is indispensable. But it is not the end of liberal politics. Principled constraints on the intrusiveness of public institutions are only one of several means to liberal citizenship. As individuals increasingly internalize liberal values, they will need constitutional safeguards to an ever diminishing degree. A community populated by such persons could afford progressively to lessen liberal constraints on democratic collective choice, without fear that liberal values will be transgressed. This is the goal. The way to advance toward it, now and for the foreseeable future, is neither to retract democracy, as liberal democrats do, nor to withdraw liberal protections, as radical democrats have too often supposed, but to democratize *and* liberalize to the greatest extent possible.

Faith in the possibility of a supraliberal democratic future is based on confidence in the transformative powers of democratic participation and liberal institutional arrangements. Whether such faith is justified is ultimately an empirical question, to be settled historically or, if appropriate historical initiatives are not forthcoming, never to be settled. No doubt it is wise to be skeptical of political philosophies that presuppose a transformed humankind. The (implicit) derogation of democracy that characterizes liberal democratic theory is motivated, in part, by doubts of just this sort. But participatory democrats, from Rousseau on, have insisted on the possibility of changing human beings for the better. What I would add to their speculations is the idea that liberalism too can and must be enlisted in this transformative project. Wagering, then, that liberal values can be sufficiently internalized to render liberal impediments to democratic collective choice much less necessary than they now are—it is appropriate to return to the question that launched the "equality of what" debate: what do egalitarians want? We are finally in a position to answer this question, or rather to begin to do so, from a supraliberal and therefore radically democratic perspective.

5

Democratic Equality

It was assumed throughout the "equality of what" debate that the way to distribute the right distribuand equally and to the greatest extent possible is to distribute things, external resources, to individuals. Thus it is not only re- source egalitarians who focus on resource distributions; all liberal egalitarians do. Welfare egalitarians, for example, want the resource distribution that will equalize the greatest compossible amount of welfare among individuals. The resulting distribution will differ from resource equality to the extent that people differ in the amount of welfare they derive from resources. The same holds for the other proposed distribuands: the way to bring about their equal distribu- tion, to the maximum compossible extent, is to distribute *things* to *persons*.

The focus on the private ownership of resources is, if anything, amplified at the practical level. The "equality of what" debate is about theoretical ideals. In practice, an equal distribution of any of the various distribuands proposed in the literature would be impossible to implement precisely. It can only be approxi- mated. But there is usually no way even to approximate an ideal distribution that is itself sufficiently fine-grained to discriminate between one or another contending position. Thus a good faith effort to bring about, say, welfare equal- ity will probably look very much like a good faith effort to distribute resources or any other likely distribuand equally. People do process resources into welfare or capabilities or advantages and so on differently. This fact is philosophically important. It is also relevant that individuals are differently situated in existing distributional patterns and that egalitarians are generally committed to bringing the bottom up. But the prospects for registering these facts institutionally are poor. If we could satisfactorily identify the less well off, according to whatever standard we adopt, we could compensate them differentially. But in many cases it is not feasible to do so. Very often, therefore, the only practical way that is also morally acceptable even to approximate the equal distribution of any proposed distribuand would be to distribute a subset of resources, income and wealth, equally or nearly equally (taking special needs into account). Then, since private property and markets are assumed throughout the "equality of what" literature, liberal egalitarian proposals, at the practical level, amount to proposals to *redistribute* market-generated distributions of income and wealth. It is ironic that after exploding the reigning pre-analytic intuition about equality, namely, that egalitarians want everyone to have the same things, the "equality of what" literature effectively reintroduces this understanding at the level of institutional design. Since the proxy distribuands—income and wealth—are equally divisible and universally desirable, egalitarians are institutionally, though not theoretically, committed to the "dogma" Dworkin (1981b) long ago disparaged: "to each the same"—that is, the same (or nearly the same) income and wealth. Of course, this commitment is only a concession to the practical difficulties inherent in the equal distribution of the right distribuand, whatever it may be. But it is revealing nevertheless, for it is even more salient at the practical level than at the level of ideal theory that liberal egalitarianism is concerned, in the main, with *individuals'* holdings of external *things*.

Both components of this assumption merit attention. Thus it is supposed that equal shares attach to individuals, in other words that the way to accord equal respect to persons is to regard individuals as ciphers to whom are allotted equal amounts of the right distribuand—or, if this is impossible in practice, equal shares of the proxy distribuands, income and wealth. And it is assumed that the right way to achieve the desired outcome, whatever it may be, is through a particular distribution of things to individuals. The former claim reflects the deep individualism of modern moral philosophy. It is closely related to the conviction that underlies the presumption for equality itself, the belief in the moral equality of persons, and it is probably as insusceptible to further justification. The latter assumption, however, is quite vulnerable. In what follows I exploit some of these vulnerabilities in order to push egalitarianism in a supraliberal direction. To this end I endeavor to restore some long-standing connections between egalitarianism and socialism. Doing so will connect the critique of liberal egalitarianism, broached in Chapter 2, with the reflections on political liberalism and liberal democracy developed in Chapters 3 and 4.

We saw in Chapter 4 that the tension between liberalism and democracy, evident to all observers in the early years of their coexistence, survives under liberal democracy, though liberal democratic institutions obscure it and liberal democratic theory hardly acknowledges it. This tension carries over to liberal egalitarianism, too, in ways that are not quite so apparent. In support of this claim, I will question the assumptions of the "equality of what" debate. I will not challenge the idea that individuals are the fundamental units for egalitarian concern. To forsake that idea is to give up deeply entrenched ways of thinking about the justification of social and political arrangements, according to which it is necessary (and perhaps also sufficient) for legitimate institutions to accord with the deepest fundamental interests of the individuals they affect. What I question instead is the idea that, to realize egalitarian aims, it suffices to distribute things to persons. Resource equality is a live contender in the "equality of what" literature, and all parties rely on resource distribution as at least an indirect means for implementing the ideals they uphold. That they are right to do so is, for all practical purposes, beyond dispute. But the fullest possible egalitarian vision cannot be realized, I argue, solely through the distribution of privately owned things. Equal respect for moral personality cannot fail to involve as well the equal distribution, to the greatest extent possible, of rights—democratic rights—to control and to benefit from the major productive assets that shape people's lives.

Thus I argue that to accommodate egalitarian aspirations fully, it is necessary to go beyond liberal equality to what I call democratic equality. To explore this idea, I resume some Rousseauian themes introduced in Chapter 4 and also reflect on some of Marx's ideas about ideal social arrangements. It will become plain that democratic equality involves not only the transcendence of liberalism, an idea already implicit in Rousseauian political philosophy, but also the extension of the Rousseauian model of democratic citizenship into areas of social and economic life that are effectively out of bounds for liberal democrats and liberal egalitarians. It is for this reason that democratic equality implies the end of the regime of private property that liberal egalitarians assume.

What I have to say about democratic equality and especially about its connections with socialism and communism (small c) must, of course, remain speculative and incomplete. One reason why has already been indicated: the case for transcending liberal horizons depends on faith in the transformative effects of liberal and democratic institutions. Such faith is reasonable but not incontrovertible; and inasmuch as the existing evidence that bears on this question is scant and equivocal, there is no prospect of justifying this faith definitively at this time. In addition, the demise of Communism (big C) has forced recognition of what ought to have been realized a long time ago: that extant understandings of alternatives to capitalist property relations are woefully inadequate. This shortcoming of traditional and contemporary social philosophy and socialist theory is yet to be rectified. There is no choice, therefore, but to rely on received understandings of social property, the term I shall use generically to designate alternatives to private property. This situation too gives what follows a necessarily underdeveloped and tentative cast. But despite these reservations, it is fair to conclude that what supraliberal egalitarians want is democratic equality. What follows, then, is a series of related attempts to clarify and defend a notion, democratic equality, that existing theory suggests but that only future developments, both practical and theoretical, can fully elaborate and vindicate.

There is a sense in which democratic equality, because it joins egalitarianism to democratic theory, is even more removed from intuitive understandings of equality than liberal equality. But it is nevertheless likely that pre-analytic intuitions about equality would be more nearly satisfied in a democratic egalitarian regime than in a liberal egalitarian one. The intuitive idea, again, is that the right distribuand should be distributed equally, and to the greatest extent possible, to all individuals. Liberal egalitarianism, in all of its versions, requires deviations from outcome equality—for the sake of holding individuals responsible for the distributional consequences of their free choices. Democratic equality implicitly relaxes this constraint. In the conditions under which it becomes an appropriate ideal, reasons of justice no longer block outcome equality. Of course, other considerations may still stand in the way of strictly equal distributions of the right distribuand. But these factors are almost certainly less severe in their intuitively inegalitarian consequences than liberal egalitarianism's defining conviction. I have already remarked on the irony that outcome equality becomes normatively feasible only after the circumstances of justice recede and distributional questions take on a diminished moral urgency. We can now identify a related irony. As we advance along a trajectory that distances us increasingly from what egalitarians pre-reflectively believe—proceeding first to liberal equality and then *beyond* it—we find ourselves very nearly back where we began, with distributions effectively governed by the principle "to each the same."

In order to clarify and defend what I mean by democratic equality, I begin by distinguishing it from the notions of *political equality,* which all liberals acknowledge, and *equality of political influence.* I then offer some considerations that bear on socialism and communism (small *c*). Here I am concerned particularly with the political implications of commitments to these ways of organizing social and economic life. This focus clears the way for resuming the discussion of Rousseauian understandings of democratic citizenship and democratic community. By bringing socialism and communism back into egalitarian theory, it becomes possible, finally, to put Rousseau's ideas to work in the task of rethinking the egalitarian project. I will then conclude by reflecting briefly on some affinities between democratic equality and intuitive understandings of egalitarian aims, and on the practical and philosophical implications of these connections.

Political Equality and Equal Political Influence

At least since the French Revolution, all strains of political theory that are not literally "reactionary" with respect to the spirit and letter of the *Declaration of the Rights of Man* have endorsed the idea of political equality, equality of citizenship.[1] Thus there is widespread support for such ideas as one person one vote, equality under the law, and, in more progressive liberal democratic regimes, equal provision of certain welfare rights.[2] This ideal has been widely transgressed. One need only recall the protracted struggles waged in almost all liberal democracies to extend the franchise to non–property holders, to women, and to members of racial minorities. However, partisans in these struggles could always appeal rhetorically to the idea of political equality and to the official consensus around that value. Despite a long-standing tension between theory and practice in the dominant political ideologies of the modern period, there can be little doubt that *at least in theory* everyone agrees that citizens qua citizens have a legitimate claim for equal treatment by the state. Thus, within the liberal democratic tradition, the eventual extension of the franchise to all citizens finally brought practice in line with long-established theoretical convictions. Liberalism requires the full and equal provision of citizenship rights. This claim is clearly evident, for example, in Rawls's (1971) contention that justice requires the equal provision of basic rights and liberties to the greatest extent possible, and in his insistence that this requirement be accorded lexical priority over other demands of justice.

A commitment to equal citizenship rights is hardly specific to liberalism. The idea is central to any political theory engaged, however tenuously, in the "emancipatory" project that Marx (1964) and his fellow Young Hegelians simultaneously embraced and faulted. Marx's claim, most evident in his *On the Jewish Question* (1843), implies that although political emancipation—specifically, the full accordance of citizenship rights to Jews and other minorities—was laudable and progressive, it effectively "displaced" and even intensified "alienation" throughout civil society. Implicit in this claim was the idea that a regime based on political equality, a *Rechtstaat,* superintends and reinforces even more fundamental inequalities generated by the economic structure it sustains. Therefore, Marx maintained, political emancipation requires full and genuine "human emancipation" if it is finally to be "complete." Marx did not level this critique of political equality just at his liberal contemporaries. He considered the commitment to political equality a legacy of the Enlightenment and its political expression, the French Revolution. As such, it was emblematic of modern political thought. Rejecting it outright—in contrast to going *beyond* it, as he sought to do—was therefore tantamount to rejecting most of the advances registered in politics and law since the inception of the nation-state and the concurrent (and not unrelated) entry of the *demos* into the political arena.

---

[1] Some nineteenth-century antirevolutionaries like Bonald and deMaistre therefore fall outside the consensus view, as do defenders of fascism and related doctrines in the twentieth century.

[2] The case for including welfare rights was articulated long ago by Richard Tawney (1931).

One theme that emerges from Marx's reflections on these themes is the idea that formal citizenship rights are necessary, but not sufficient, for assuring that citizens engage in political processes on an equal basis. Like equality of opportunity, political equality can be understood in a purely formal sense; it can be held to obtain whenever legal and customary impedances in its way are removed. Or it can be held that political equality exists only when citizenship rights are accorded what Rawls calls their "fair value," in other words when individuals actually have the means necessary for rendering their rights exercisable. Following Rawls's lead, liberal egalitarians generally favor the latter understanding.

I will focus, for now, on only one aspect of political equality so conceived: equality in the determination of collective choices. To the extent that democratic theorists have come to identify democracy with collective choice rules, this is a position to which democrats are inevitably led. If only implicitly, they are proponents of *equality of political influence.*

Equality of political influence, to the greatest compossible extent, represents the fundamental democratic aspiration for rule of, by, and for the people, filtered through the individualist prism of modern moral and political theory. We know that originally democracy meant rule by the popular masses, the *demos.* But if we allow that the individual ought to be abstracted away from class and other group identifications, then the old idea is tantamount to a commitment to accord equal weight to each individual in the determination of political outcomes. It is this understanding that motivates the now familiar view of democracy as a collective choice rule, a method for aggregating individuals' choices, where each individual's "input" counts equally in the determination of the "output," the social choice, and where the social choice is exclusively a function of individuals' choices for the alternatives in contention.

Even the most dedicated proponents of this model of democratic decision making, however, should appreciate the force of a countervailing intuition, according to which it is wrong to require individuals to participate in political activities when they do not want to do so. If only for this reason, it is best not to represent the democratic ideal as equality of political influence but as *equal opportunity* for political influence.[3] Then institutions are democratic to the extent that they allow individuals to be equally influential in collective decision making and other political processes, should they choose to exercise their opportunities for political influence fully.

Needless to say, so long as political institutions are hierarchically structured, incumbents of high offices will generally be able to affect outcomes to a greater degree than incumbents of lesser offices, who will in turn have more effect on outcomes than ordinary citizens. Proponents of equal opportunity for political

[3] A related idea is defended in Brighouse 1996.

influence are obliged to take account of this inevitable fact of political life. Rousseau (1762) accommodated this inevitability by distinguishing the sovereign, that is, the people themselves, from the government. The sovereign legislates; the government executes the sovereign's will. Obviously, incumbents of government positions affect outcomes more than other citizens do; they literally bring outcomes about. But in the state Rousseau envisioned, they have no greater control over the outcome of legislation than anyone else. In that crucial sense, the existence of government is compatible with equal opportunity for political influence. Democratic theorists who take issue with Rousseau's positions on direct democracy and on the subordination of executive to legislative functions, but who nevertheless rally behind the idea of equal opportunity for political influence, are obliged to concoct a functionally equivalent rationale. I will not pursue this issue at this point except to register the opinion that equal opportunity for political influence, properly analyzed and qualified, is almost certainly a coherent ideal. Political hierarchies in democratic states do not embarrass the idea of equal opportunity for political influence than they embarrass the related idea of rule by an undifferentiated citizenry.

The idea of equal opportunity for political influence does not figure as a candidate distribuand in the "equality of what" debate in quite the same way that, say, resource equality or welfare equality do. The idea belongs to democratic theory, and, as it happens, liberal egalitarians are almost always also democrats—indeed, liberal democrats. But within the parameters of the "equality of what" literature, egalitarian and democratic commitments usually remain separate. Equal opportunity for political influence strains this separation. In doing so, the concept anticipates the reconceptualization of democratic and egalitarian concerns that is critical for transcending the horizons of liberal egalitarianism altogether.

Equal opportunity for political influence can entail equality along other dimensions as well. But this is so only because political influence is affected by nonpolitical circumstances, especially by the distribution of income and wealth. Thus it seems plain that once formal political equality is assured, the way to distribute opportunities for political influence equally is through an equal—or nearly equal—distribution of income and wealth. But it is almost inevitable that income and wealth inequalities spill over into the political sphere. In principle, it should be possible to insulate political institutions from economic inequalities—say, by public financing of candidates for elective offices and proscriptions on certain types of "lobbying." Thus, in theory, equal opportunity for political influence is compatible with income and wealth inequality. In practice, however, because economic inequalities do spill over into the political sphere extensively and ubiquitously, the goal of equal opportunity for political influence has strongly redistributive implications.

Even so, equal opportunity for political influence poses no deep challenge to liberal democratic institutions or to their justifying theories. Indeed, the civic culture of liberal democracies actively promotes the illusion that equality of political influence already largely exists. This belief is plainly useful for sustaining the de facto legitimacy of existing regimes in a world in which democratic aspirations run deep. The recognition that opportunities for political influence are unequally distributed embarrasses defenders of the system in place, even while they ignore the implications of what they perceive, and even while they embrace practices that generate the inequalities they decry. Similarly, unequal treatment, say, of individuals of different races or socioeconomic groups in courts of law embarrasses proponents of political equality, even while they participate in and benefit from inequalities of legal treatment. The only way for partisans of these values to countenance situations of this sort is to turn a blind eye to them. Where equal opportunity for political influence is in question, citizens of liberal democracies seem especially prone to self-deception or willful denial. This is why the concept is a potentially critical, even radical, standard against which the real world of liberal democracy can be assessed. Its vigorous promotion can force liberal democrats to acknowledge the very radical implications of their own theoretical convictions—putting a host of existing practices and institutional arrangements in question. In this respect, equal opportunity for political influence is like neutrality (see Chapter 1). But again, like neutrality, the idea poses no fundamental challenge either to liberal egalitarianism or to liberal democracy. It only articulates what proponents of these positions already implicitly accept, whether they realize it or not.

In contrast, democratic equality exceeds the limits of liberal theory and practice. The idea includes political equality and equal opportunity for political influence, but it also suggests a social order beyond these desiderata. It *incorporates* the values liberals defend at the same time that it *transcends* the horizons of liberalism itself.

Private Property and Socialism

I have already suggested that to move beyond liberal egalitarianism, it is necessary to blunt the force of the idea that what matters, for equality, is the distribution of *privately* owned things. Before the recent eclipse of socialist theory and politics, the idea that there is an alternative to private ownership seemed unexceptionable. But this is no longer the case. Nowadays almost everyone, including of course liberal egalitarians, accept notions of property specific to capitalism. This turn of events is uncalled for and unnecessary. The question of socialism can and should return to the forefront of egalitarian concerns.

For nearly two centuries, "socialism" has been used in a variety of ways, not always consistently and not always clearly. Nearly always, however, the term designates, at the very least, an economic system in which major productive assets are owned socially, not privately. Although the difference between social and private ownership is not as clear as it once was, we can nevertheless identify many cases of private ownership unproblematically. Thus it is beyond dispute that nearly all productive enterprises in the United States and in other capitalist countries, especially after the recent worldwide wave of "privatizations," are privately owned. Assuming a secure enough understanding of what private ownership is, we can define social ownership as its negation. Let us assume, furthermore, that whatever is not privately owned is socially owned, allowing that there may be cases that are difficult to classify—for example, varieties of state ownership in both capitalist and formerly "socialist" societies. With this admittedly inadequate understanding of social ownership in place, we can say that a society is socialist if and only if its principal means of production are socially owned. This usage has a bona fide Marxist or, at least, historical materialist pedigree.[4] It therefore provides a familiar purchase on private property and socialism. We will see, however, that this understanding of socialism can divert attention from important insights—some of them also of a generally Marxian provenance—about what egalitarians ultimately want. Marxists, like everyone else, have been overly categorical in distinguishing social from private property. Despite all the attention they have paid to "social relations of production," they have *undertheorized* property. This theoretical deficit remains unremedied. Nevertheless, the fate of socialist theory and, indeed, of many of the deepest issues in social philosophy today depend on developing a more nuanced understanding of property relations. I cannot pursue this enormous and largely uncharted project very far here. But, with received understandings as my point of departure, I will take a few tentative steps toward rectifying this vast deficit in the egalitarian's theoretical arsenal.

If socialism were nothing more than an economic system in which property rights are socialized (deprivatized), it is hard to see how it could ever have been sought *for its own sake,* much less how socialism could serve as an ideal that elicits deep political passions. Thus one might be tempted to conclude that the socialization (deprivatization) of a society's principal means of production is only a means to other ends and that, wittingly or not, socialists do not want socialism per se but rather something that it is more reasonable to value intrinsically, something for which socialist property relations are indispensable or, at least, instrumental in a pertinent range of circumstances. An obvious suggestion is that what socialists have always wanted is equality, and that they have been socialists because they were egalitarians. John Roemer (1994) has advanced precisely this claim. In Roemer's view, socialists are, in fact, liberal egalitarians, committed to equalizing some combination of the

---

[4] I defend this contention in Levine 1988, 1987.

most likely distribuands proposed in the "equality of what" literature.[5] They differ from other liberal egalitarians only insofar as they are committed to a view about the efficacy of socialist property relations for advancing egalitarian aims. But there are no differences in fundamental valuational commitments between socialists and liberals who defend (or simply assume) capitalist property rights. In Roemer's view, prosocialist and procapitalist liberal egalitarians ultimately want the same thing.

To assess this contention, it will be useful once again to focus on politics, specifically the politics implicit in commitments to one or the other form of ownership. What has been the aim of *socialist* politics? What has motivated the struggle to socialize (or at least deprivatize) property rights in major productive assets? The most comprehensive answer, surely, is that socialists, with few exceptions, have been anticapitalists. They have opposed capitalist civilization and favored an alternative, distinctively *social,* vision of ideal economic, social, and political arrangements. Despite some reservations by Marxists, motivated mainly by polemical concerns, the socialist vision plainly includes equality. Thus Roemer is surely right in part. But only in part. It will be instructive to reflect on that part briefly before turning to what Roemer leaves out.

It is plain how socialism is instrumental for equality. Privately owned productive assets generate revenues that accrue to the individuals who own them, and these revenue streams can differ significantly in magnitude, especially when ownership rights themselves are unequally distributed. One way to eliminate these inequalities is to attack them at their source. The deprivatization of productive assets eliminates this source of economic and social inequality in capitalist societies. Of course, the private ownership of productive assets is not the only cause of income inequalities under capitalism. Eliminating this inequality-generating mechanism will therefore not eliminate income inequality as such. Under capitalism (and perhaps under socialism too) it is almost always expedient, for efficiency reasons, to provide differential material rewards for the exercise of talent and effort. There may also be unavoidable efficiency reasons for providing differential rewards to incumbents of offices in hierarchically structured institutions. Therefore, under conditions of (near) abundance, when efficiency concerns effectively cease to matter, there may be no feasible long-term substitutes for material incentives.[6] But the inequalities endemic to capitalism

---

[5] Thus Roemer maintains that equal opportunity for self-realization and welfare, for political influence, and for social status is what socialists have always wanted. He does not say how these distribuands should be combined in cases of conflict. See also Levine 1996a.

[6] There are alternatives, however, especially in the short term. Coercion is one. But setting aside *moral* objections to the use of coercion as a way of extracting labor inputs, it is evident that material incentives generally work better from an efficiency standpoint. Where there are voluntary labor inputs motivated by differential material rewards, fewer resources must be put to use in the surveillance and supervision of labor, and workers themselves are likely to be more productive. This is one reason why capitalism develops what Marx called "forces of production" more rapidly than those

are only partly explained by this exigency. The principal source of social and economic inequalities under capitalism is what is distinctive to capitalism itself, the private ownership of productive assets. To eliminate this defining feature of capitalist economic structures is therefore to strike a powerful blow for egalitarian aims.

But the abolition of private ownership of productive assets is not strictly necessary for eliminating inequalities, including inequalities generated by private ownership. Insofar as the point is to equalize incomes, redistributive taxation and national (or international) wage policies will do as well or better, at least in principle. We might also imagine mechanisms for redistributing privately owned productive assets directly, allowing the revenues they generate to fall where they may—provided of course that it is done in a way that promotes efficiency or at least meets reasonable expectations about economic performance. But capitalism with an egalitarian face is not what socialists want. This is not because socialists are unclear about their objectives or confuse ends and means. It is because the socialist tradition's purchase on equality implies a vision of social arrangements with which capitalism is ultimately incompatible, no matter how egalitarian capitalist societies become. Socialist anticapitalism is a principled position, not a conceptual confusion or a historical accident. The idea that socialists are really only liberal egalitarians represents, I believe, a well-intentioned effort to maintain socialism as an ideal in the face of its apparent demise. But it is unwise and unnecessary to destroy socialism in order to save it.

I would suggest that any attempt at dissolving socialism into something else on the grounds that it is only a means to some other end is wrong-headed. I also would venture that clear-headed socialists have always understood that socialized (deprivatized) property is desirable because it is *instrumental* for other ends. But it does not follow automatically that, for these socialists, socialism would be dispensable if a more efficacious means to attain the desired ends were found. The ends envisioned in at least some strains of the socialist tradition and the means through which they are to be realized are too closely joined to be severed. For the socialists I have in mind, the end that socialism serves is *social,* not merely political, citizenship—a community of free and equal social citizens. To establish a community of this sort, the socialization (deprivatization) of property relations is not just instrumental but indispensable.

One can endorse this vision and still believe that at particular levels of economic development capitalism is better than any imaginable form of socialism

---

modes of production that rely on coercion (feudalism, for example). This historical materialist truism is amply born out by a host of historical examples—from slavery in the American South to the widespread use of terror during the Stalin period in the former Soviet Union. Moral incentives are another alternative. But their successful deployment depends on a degree of heroism that is almost certainly impossible to sustain over long periods of time.

for delivering the goods people want and facilitating the expansion of productive capacities, in other words for creating the material conditions needed to realize the socialist vision. In this case, the end in view would have to wait until productive capacities have sufficiently matured. Then there would be at least a prima facie case for avoiding socialist means to socialist ends. This is, in fact, what some socialists have recommended for their own time and place. Social citizenship may also be impossible unless certain noneconomic conditions hold. Especially from a perspective that emphasizes the transformation of individuals' characters, political institutions and cultural practices are at least as crucial for realizing the socialist vision as property relations. Means to socialist ends must therefore be assessed from this vantage-point as well. But however the assessment goes, socialists cannot dispense with socialism forever. Ultimately, socialism itself—or rather what socialism can become—is what socialists want.

The idea of social citizenship received its clearest evocation in Marx's concept of communism, an idea fraught with difficulties, but also pregnant with indications of a different and better future than anything imaginable from within a liberal egalitarian purview. What socialists want, I maintain, is not liberal equality but *communism*, a regime of free (uncoerced) social citizenship. Communist societies, communities of social citizens, *transcend* liberal democracy and liberal equality as well. They instantiate democratic equality. Thus communism is what egalitarians want too.

communism

Nowadays, communism (small *c*) is almost universally thought to be a utopian ideal that cannot possibly be realized. If this understanding is sound, then perhaps egalitarian aspirations ought indeed to stop with liberal equality, and perhaps liberal equality is all that would-be socialists should seek. Whether or not to pursue this end in a socialist manner by transforming property relations would then depend solely on assessments of socialism's efficacy, relative to alternative means, in promoting liberal equality, just as Roemer maintains. Socialism, after all, is not integral to liberal equality in the way that it is to the more robust ideal of communism—an ideal that, I maintain, egalitarians ought to uphold.

The consensus today about a feasible society stops far short of communism. It stops effectively at the reform of capitalism and liberal democracy. This perception bears witness to the end of an aspiration that has sustained a large portion of humankind for more than two centuries: the hope of rationally administering human affairs to meet human needs. It is now widely believed that the greatest attainable rationality is the rationality of the economic agent. At the societal level, therefore, the best we can expect is the elimination or at least the mitigation of unintended, suboptimal consequences of individuals' maximizing choices, through the workings of "the invisible hand." This goal is a pale shadow of the old aspiration to establish a genuinely rational social order. But if attempts at rationalizing economic and social affairs directly are bound to fail, perhaps that is all we can reasonably expect.

This pessimistic judgment is nowadays more often celebrated than bemoaned. No doubt part of the explanation has to do with the glorification of market mechanisms that has spread from sectors of the economics profession into the broader intellectual and political culture. Since markets are driven by individual optimizing choices, and since such optimizing is all the rationality we can (safely) obtain, we are indeed well advised to rely on markets—not as temporary expedients but forever. The debate then centers on whether market "incompetencies"—in producing public goods and controlling externalities—and other features of markets that detract from overall efficiency can be countered by the introduction of yet additional market mechanisms or, if not, on how to concoct public sector remedies that will not unduly burden the market-driven economy. Who can remain unaffected by this revolution of diminishing expectations! In a world in which even affirmative state liberalism has come to seem misguided if not quaint, communism is off the political agenda altogether.

It is also fair to observe that the self-proclaimed realism that has lately become so pervasive is partly a reaction to the demise of Communism (big *C*). But the facts hardly sustain the conclusion. The economic system of the former Soviet Union and the regimes that followed its lead did differ significantly from those in place in the Western democracies. It is worth recalling that, for many decades, the Soviet system seemed viable and, from an economic point of view, even superior to its capitalist rivals. This is one reason why the Soviet Union was a model for economic development, not just in those parts of the world that it dominated, but also throughout much of the so-called Third World. Moreover, the Soviet Union did have a socialist economy in the sense that its principal means of production were socially (not privately) owned. But the values democrats and liberals seek to implement were even less realized in the Communist world than in the Western liberal democracies. The problem was not just political or even social. To be sure, the political structures of the former Soviet Union and the countries it influenced were hardly democratic. Those regimes were manifestly illiberal too, and the social mores that Soviet-style political structures encouraged were no more conducive to enhancing the moral equality of persons than the traditional mores they (only partially) supplanted. Thus, as revolutionary upheavals subsided in the Soviet Union, traditional patterns of social relations reasserted themselves, often with the encouragement of the political regime. Similar conditions were installed elsewhere in the Soviet bloc without even the historical memory of a revolutionary "moment" when genuinely freer and more solidary ways of organizing social life were at hand. But the blame for the collapse of this alternative to capitalism cannot be attributed to politics and culture alone. The problem was also economic, resonating all the way down to the nature of property relations themselves.

Before the October Revolution, socialists, including Marxists, had hardly even broached questions about the nature and (possible) forms of social property. Thus there was effectively no socialist economic theory. Postrevolutionary socialists were therefore obliged to improvise. Too often, they did so unimaginatively. They took it for granted that social (deprivatized) property was state property, and they assumed that state property could be put to best use through centralized, bureaucratic administration, modeled on the economies of Germany and other belligerent states during the First World War. Today, many of the shortcomings of these assumptions are well understood.[7] We therefore have at least a passable understanding of Communism's failings—gauged not only by capitalist standards, but on its own terms as well.

It is not at all clear, however, why the failure of Communism should cause communism (small c) to fall into disrepute; for apart from its self-representations, Communism had very little to do with the Marxian ideal. The name was the same—in part because the very first Communists probably were communists, in part because Marxism became a useful legitimating ideology for Communist regimes. But apart from these historical contingencies, Communism is almost entirely irrelevant to the issues in contention here. At most, what it shows is what was already abundantly clear: however necessary the deprivatization of ownership of productive assets may be for obtaining what socialists want, it is by no means sufficient. This lesson aside, a historical assessment of the history of Communism is unlikely to illuminate much about communism's feasibility or normative standing.

What then is communism? Marx himself was deliberately unforthcoming on this question, preferring not to predict what genuinely free men and women would choose to do, individually and collectively, in a radically democratized regime. He insisted that there is no way to tell with any specificity what will happen as historical tendencies unfold and human beings finally do assume control of those aspects of their lives that genuinely are of their own contrivance. Nevertheless Marx did offer a few general prognostications that his successors have made canonical. It will be useful to consider some of them here in order to reflect upon their implications for democratic equality.

Perhaps the best-known of Marx's characterizations of communism is his claim that individuals living in communist societies will contribute to social wealth according to their abilities, and that distributions—of exactly what distribuand is unclear—will then be according to need.[8] Full-fledged communism contrasts with socialism, its "first stage," where individuals' shares are distrib-

---

[7] For a comprehensive account, see Kornai 1992.

[8] See Marx, *Critique of the Gotha Program,* in Marx and Engels 1962, 2:24.

uted in proportion to their productive contributions, determined by the amount of socially necessary labor time they expend. Marx's rationale is clear: at the level of economic and cultural development reached at the time socialism is introduced, principles of "bourgeois right" must remain in effect—in order to maintain an incentive structure conducive to further economic development. Under communism, it will no longer be necessary to rely on this expedient. However, it is misleading to construe the principle "from each according to ability, to each according to need"—the slogan Marx would have communist society "inscribe on its banners"—as a substantive principle of justice, analogous to the socialist principle "to each according to productive contribution." Even allowing that we could somehow ascertain abilities and needs uncontroversially, it would be ungenerous to hold Marx to the view that it is fair, in conditions of abundance, for individuals to contribute in proportion to their abilities and receive what is produced in proportion to their needs. Before anything like the communist slogan can be inscribed on society's banners and put into effect by its economic institutions, the circumstances of justice must first fade away. As they do so, fairness matters less, and distributional principles, whatever their content, lose their urgency. Thus it is with "to each according to need." It is not so much a principle of justice as a description of the way that goods and services would be produced and distributed after fairness—and efficiency too—have ceased to matter in the way they do while scarcity reigns.

Were the principle that is supposed to govern distributions under communism a substantive principle of justice, it would fall short on both efficiency and equity grounds. The efficiency problem is that the system of incentives implied by this formulation is untenable for all but unconditional altruists bent on enhancing the well-being of others irrespective of the consequences to themselves. Such people do not exist in the world as we know it. The type and degree of altruism that this principle assumes is almost certainly unsustainable, even for communist men and women. Were this formula put into effect, therefore, we could anticipate that labor would be massively underdeployed—unless, of course, individuals are forced to work against their will. The dilemma is plain: either productivity would decline precipitously or it would be necessary to implement a regime of forced labor in which individuals would lose the right not to work or to work at a level less than the amount that is optimal for generating a surplus large enough to be distributed according to need. In all likelihood, too, individuals would also lose the right to choose the nature of their employment, since they would be obliged to exercise their talents at optimal levels. It would be necessary, in short, to restrict freedom even more drastically than it is restricted in societies like our own, where the voluntarily unemployed are unsupported but where idlers who pay their own way are permitted to do as they please. In short, it would be difficult to imagine a worse way to marshal labor inputs, especially in societies intent on maintaining the freedom to work or not to work, and freedom of occupational choice.

The situation is not much better with respect to equity. Where resources are scarce, such that not everyone can have everything they want, only some goods and services can be distributed according to need. Thus it might be feasible to distribute goods that address fundamental needs in this way: some level of food, shelter, and clothing, and perhaps also medical care and other services essential for realizing the fair value of basic citizenship rights. But beyond this minimum, it is not even clear how this principle could be applied; it does not instruct us about the distribution of things that are wanted but not needed. Even if we could somehow ignore the distinction between wants and needs and distribute simply according to wants, it would be patently *unfair* to do so. Why, after all, should those who want more get more, and those who desire little become worse off on this account? Thus on equity grounds too, this principle is unacceptable—either it applies only to a comparatively small range of goods and services or else it plainly cannot pass muster.

But "from each according to ability, to each according to need" is a plausible speculation about how production and distribution would be connected in a society so affluent that fairness no longer matters very much and material incentives no longer have much effect. Affluence, again, approximates abundance, and where abundance obtains, distributional questions have no normative significance at all. Air, for example, is almost always abundant in the sense that everyone can have all they want or need at no cost to anyone else. Air is therefore free, and no one cares how large anyone else's distributive share may be. Of course, not everything can be quite like air, even in principle. As remarked in Chapter 2, so long as life itself is finite in duration, individuals will be obliged to budget their time and resources to some extent. Moreover, some goods are desirable precisely because they are scarce, while others, like being first through the door, are essentially "positional" and therefore scarce as a matter of logical necessity. Even so, abundance can be approximated. As productive forces develop, scarcity can diminish to such a degree that it would no longer be an overriding concern.

This prognostication may seem utopian, but recall that we are probably already affluent enough to disengage contribution from distribution to a very considerable extent (see Chapter 1). Communism should not be that much more demanding; communist societies would be free from late capitalism's relentless imperative to generate wants in order to sustain "effective demand." Communist societies would almost certainly not be consumer societies, at least not if Marx was right to think of human beings as self-realizers rather than consumers.[9] Relative scarcity is a function of supply relative to demand. With diminished demand and increasing supply—as consumerism gives way to a social

---

[9] See Elster 1989b.

order dedicated to self-realization and as productive capacities expand—the diminution of scarcity to benign levels is eminently likely.

Thus I would venture that it is reasonable to imagine a social order in which, as Marx says of communism, virtually all goods and services are free.[10] This is not to say that we can imagine a society—even in the remotest of futures—in which no one would work. Unlike air, most of the things people want require human effort to produce and sustain; labor inputs will therefore remain indispensable no matter how productive labor becomes. But if work will always be with us, we could, with sufficient affluence, witness the end of *toil*—work that people do because they are compelled by material circumstances or because they are forced to do so by others. We can imagine, in other words, a world in which no one is compelled to do any work they do not want to do. If we assume, following Marx, that productive labor is an essential component of the human good, necessary for self-realization, people will generally want to work.[11] Under communism, productive contributions would be motivated only by noneconomic wants of this kind. Thus "from each according to ability" does not imply that persons are obligated to contribute to the generation of a social surplus large enough to allow for the free distribution of all goods and services to everyone. It does not even imply that individuals *must* work enough to allow for the free distribution of items necessary for satisfying narrowly specified needs. Marx's idea is that, at levels of development sufficient for sustaining communism, labor sufficient for satisfying all extant—but of course not all imaginable—needs at no cost would be forthcoming solely in consequence of the free expression of each individual's nature. A sufficiency of labor would exist without recourse either to coercion or to material incentives.

Of course, for communism, so conceived, to be possible, it must be the case that the requisite level of affluence can be attained without running up against insurmountable physical limits to economic growth. In other words, for Marx to be right, Malthus (1958) must be wrong. There is no doubt that in principle there must be some upper limit to growth, if only because no human society can use up in production more natural resources or energy sources than there are to consume. But after nearly two centuries the data appear to support a view congenial to Marx's vision—that this upper limit is so high that it has no

[10] See Van Parijs 1993, chap. 10. Van Parijs observes that it is now possible to institute communism, so conceived, in two ways. First, we could ascertain, for some individuals, the level of income that would eliminate any interest they might have in working for a greater amount, and then give them that much income. Second, we could now distribute some goods and services in a communist way by making them free. We might even imagine a *gradual* transition to communism for all and everything, in the first instance by including ever more individuals into the chosen group, and in the second by including ever more goods and services. The first strategy, however, would be thoroughly unfair, the second manifestly inefficient.

[11] The clearest articulations of this view occur in Marx's early writings, especially the *1844 Paris Manuscripts* (see Marx 1964) and *The German Ideology*. See also Chapter 1 above.

significant bearing on questions of societal design. Nevertheless, the question must remain open: we do not know, with certainty, whether economic growth is possible to a degree that could sustain communism, especially at a global level. Defenders of communism can only hope that it can, and they rely on the evidence of the near and distant past to sustain their expectation. In support of this conviction, it is well to recall that under communism people have all they *actually* want without expending more effort than they freely want to expend—not all they could *possibly* want without any expenditure of effort at all.

It might also be objected that the level of economic development sufficient for communism would be ecologically devastating or would otherwise affect the quality of human and nonhuman life in ways that would render growth of this sort counterproductive or normatively undesirable or both. These "green" objections to "red" aspirations ultimately rest on empirical claims about the consequences of economic growth that are impossible to adjudicate definitively. I would only suggest that there is no reason in principle why development cannot be sound, why economic growth cannot proceed in ways that address all relevant human and nonhuman concerns. Ecological problems are real and trenchant. Marx, like all nineteenth-century thinkers, was wrongfully neglectful of them. Marxian communism was therefore conceived without according these problems their due. But it does not follow that communism cannot satisfactorily resolve them. Democratic constituencies, motivated by ecological concerns, should be able to develop productive forces wisely and ethically, according to all reasonable anthropocentric and ecocentric perspectives, provided, of course, that economic interests do not deter them from acting on these concerns. Private ownership can and does give rise to powerful counter-ecological motivations. With private ownership of major productive assets abolished or severely curtailed, the way should be clear to an ecologically sound future.

If faith in the possibility of defensible economic growth to the extent necessary for communism is justified, it is fair to attach credulity to yet another of Marx's claims—that under communism commodity production would cease. Capitalism, especially developed capitalism, commodifies voraciously; in Marx's view commodification is in fact the essence of capitalist development. But genuinely abundant things, like air, remain recalcitrant to this tendency even as the logic of capitalist development unfolds. This observation anticipates what increasing commodification portends. Like an expanding universe that reaches its physical limit and then contracts, the commodification of virtually everything must at some point undo the conditions for its own possibility. Then decommodification comes onto the historical agenda. If it is indeed capitalism's mission, as Marx believed, to develop productive forces to the point that capitalist property relations no longer serve any developmental purpose, the commodity form, generalized under capitalist conditions, is bound to become undone by its own success. Put differently, if in consequence of capitalist development there comes a time when everyone is able to do only what they want and to take whatever they please at no cost—that is, at no real cost to others and therefore at no cost to themselves—the tendency to commodify anything and everything that is socially useful will wither away for want of a sufficient reason to sustain it.

The end of commodity production implies the end of the time that exchange relations structure social life. But thereafter, of course, the need to coordinate collective endeavors will still be pressing. If nothing else, it will be necessary to organize production and distribution and generally to attend to what Engels called "the administration of things." [12] Despite what proponents of communism have also said, therefore, it is misleading to hold that under communism the state would "wither away." If by the "state" one means only what Marx sometimes intended, namely, the institutional apparatus through which an economically dominant class organizes its domination of subordinate classes and social strata, then, to be sure, communist societies would be stateless. But *administrative* exigencies are ineluctable, even under communism. The recognition of this fact points the way toward a deeper understanding of social citizenship and ultimately therefore of democratic equality itself.

Social Citizenship

When individuals seek to advance what Rousseau called their "private interests" through collective choice mechanisms, democracy is effectively a continuation of market behavior by other means. This is how the political process is conceived in the mainstream political culture. Individuals in isolation or organized into interest groups represent their interests in their votes. Voting is a mechanism for combining these representations. The voting *community*, then, is just the collection of voters. It is a community in the same sense that individuals who interact in markets comprise a community. In each case, what joins individuals together is an overriding private interest held in common. In market transactions, each party, by hypothesis, prefers a concluded exchange to an outcome in which bargaining breaks down and no exchange occurs. With voting, individuals are held together by a common but still private interest in sustaining the regime itself and its methods for arriving at collective choices. The difference is that, in voting, the common interest concerns the whole society directly; the relevant common interest exists at the "macro level." Participants in markets typically want the market system itself to survive and therefore have a common macro-level interest too. But the relevant common interest that makes market transactions possible exists at the level of the exchange itself. Markets, again, are just agglomerations of individual transactions. They generate social choices, but

[12] Marx and Engels 1962, 2:150–53.

only indirectly, as unintended consequences of micro-level exchanges. In both cases, however, within the space created by common interests, there is a struggle for competitive advantage; everyone is in competition with everyone else. All sides aim to win—not, however, as in a state of nature, where there are no rules whatsoever, but against a background of (possibly implicit) agreements that regulate the terms in which contending parties compete. Needless to say, this picture contrasts sharply with Rousseau's idea, according to which voting is a procedure aimed at discovering a genuine consensus on ends. For Rousseau, it is not enough that everyone agree on the rules of the game. Everyone must also want the same thing, the general interest, even if they disagree, as people will in particular cases, about what the general interest is.

This alternative view supports a notion of community that warrants further reflection. Political theorists generally assume that the idea of community is exogenous to democracy. It is sometimes acknowledged that an awareness of a common destiny or shared experience—maintained horizontally, across individuals, and vertically, across generations—generates and sustains "metapreferences" for observing the rules of the game. Thus it is widely believed that some measure of community is indispensable for maintaining stable political institutions, that self-interest alone is not enough. But community, so conceived, remains conceptually if not causally independent of democracy. In the Rousseauian model, on the other hand, community and democracy are integrally joined. Voting discovers the general will because there exists a consensus on ends, because each person qua citizen wants the same thing. The idea, then, is not that private interests converge or that social choices represent unanimous preferences. Rather, it is that membership in the voting community implies putting the interests of that community—or rather one's own interests as a member of that "moral and collective body"—above one's private interests. Votes represent *opinions* about what the general interest is, not *preferences* for alternative outcomes in contention. Individuals are "experts" in ascertaining what the general will is because it is their own, insofar as they are citizens. Rousseau insisted, of course, that the truth is found by counting the votes. But that truth is already present in each citizen. Voting therefore only discovers what is potentially (though fallibly) accessible by introspection alone.[13] It does not *constitute* the general will. It reveals it.

On this view, it is a consensus on ends that draws individuals together. The community exists because individuals want the same thing—the general interest, the good for "the whole community" of which they are an integral part. In communal deliberations and in voting, citizens discover what they want; they

---

[13] Rousseau's claim that majorities are better able than individuals themselves to discover what each individual qua citizen truly wants is asserted without argument. But this (initially implausible) contention can in fact be supported by good, if not overwhelming, arguments, as I explain in Levine 1976, 63–72.

discover what the general interest is. Or rather they discover what it is insofar as they deliberate and vote as fully equal members of the "moral and collective body" they constitute. Thus, for Rousseau, equality, democracy, and community are related more intimately than they are in the mainstream view. These values are each different expressions of the same notional fact, the reality of democratic equality. Marxian communism is, in this crucial respect, a thoroughly Rousseauian idea.

For reasons already discussed, under communism liberal constraints are effectively *incorporated* into each citizen's deliberations. If it should turn out that liberal institutional arrangements must remain in force, even under communist conditions, it could only mean that that people remain morally recalcitrant: individuals are not able fully to accept their roles as equal members of freely constituted democratic egalitarian communities. But even so, liberal institutions would not be morally required at the level of ideal theory. They would be concessions to human unreason, reminders of what even democratic egalitarian communities must strive, perhaps in vain, to overcome.

In a supraliberal world, with the need for liberal constitutional constraints diminished and the rationale for their existence fundamentally changed, the characteristic liberal division between the state and civil society could hardly survive intact. The boundaries between them would inevitably blur. Is this consequence, the "transcendence" of liberalism, something that partisans of equal treatment ought to regret? It might seem so, for it has become part of the common sense of our political culture that a strong civil society insulates citizens from illegitimate political interferences and stands as a bulwark against tyranny. I will not fault this assessment. It is a conclusion that the political history of the past century forces on the consciousness of even the most "utopian" egalitarian. But it is hardly a decisive objection to democratic equality. Like constitutional constraints themselves and for much the same reason, the liberal state/civil society division matters to the extent that liberal norms are not already internalized in the citizens they govern. A community of genuinely social citizens would therefore have little to fear and much to gain from the *politicization* of civil society. The point is not just that individuals' (transformed) characters would render the threat of totalitarian usurpations of individuals' rights benign while expanding the scope of democratic collective choice. It is rather that the collapse of the traditional state/civil society distinction under communism presupposes the *transformation* of both the state and civil society in ways that are likely to obviate the threat of tyranny.

Because my topic is equality, I will not say more here about likely changes in the nature of the state; nor will I speculate about transformations in nonstate societal institutions that have no direct bearing on egalitarian distributions. But I cannot conclude this section without returning briefly to the question of socialism, because social property is key to the development of social citizenship and therefore to the realization of democratic equality. It should be plain by now that however serviceable it has been to regard social property as an antonym of private property, the lack of a full-fledged theory of social property is ultimately unsatisfactory. A fuller account of social community and therefore of democratic equality awaits a richer understanding of alternatives to capitalist property relations. Nevertheless, even the bare idea of deprivatization affords some insight into how democratic egalitarian aspirations might be realized. What we can see, even now, is that egalitarians should abandon the assumption that the *principal* and perhaps the *only* way to implement egalitarian aims is to assign particular distributions of things to persons. For a community of equal social citizens to exist, *ownership* of everything vital to the whole community— including, emphatically, the society's major productive assets—must be in the hands of those who are principally affected by their operation. Thus some form of workers' control of enterprises and of societal control of productive investment is almost certainly called for. It is also plain that to some extent the income streams that productive assets generate should redound to the benefit of the entire "moral and collective body" these assets serve.

Some delegation of authority in these matters, from the people to their agents, may often be expedient, in part for efficiency reasons (insofar as efficiency considerations remain pertinent) and in part to free citizens from the burdens of governance. But, ultimately, authority over the principal economic aspects of the erstwhile civil society must remain in the hands of the people themselves, and therefore subject to democratic control. In other words, the model of citizenship that Rousseau introduced with respect to the *state,* according to which individuals *directly* legislate the rules under which they live, should be extended to apply within the economic sphere. Exactly how a generalization of Rousseauian citizenship might be implemented institutionally must remain obscure, awaiting the rectification of a number of salient theoretical deficits in the socialist tradition, including, above all, a rethinking of the idea of social property itself. But in a general way we can already see that socialism implies a focus quite remote from the concerns of the "equality of what" literature. The socialization (deprivatization) of society's principal means of production gives rise to a concern with the distribution of rights to govern socially owned things, to control their use, and to benefit from their deployment. From this perspective, what egalitarians want is bound to involve the reassignment of revenue and control rights over (important) productive assets. For supraliberal egalitarians, therefore, the nature and distribution of such rights within a transformed body politic will be of as much or greater concern than the distribution of things to individuals.

Democratic equality therefore consists in the extension of Rousseauian citizenship to erstwhile social and economic aspects of human life, a feat that is barely conceivable and utterly unfeasible from within the purview of liberal democratic theory and practice. The politicization of those aspects of civil society that pertain to economic matters is a necessary step to this end. But this step is impossible to take, or rather to take safely, until liberal institutional constraints are internalized by democratic citizens. As I have said, the prospects for a genuinely transformative politics must, for now, remain an open question. But it is fair to say, even so, that a condition for the possibility of bringing *desirable* transformations about is the democratization of ownership and control rights over important productive assets—in other words, the abolition of private property in society's principal means of production. So long as private property is assumed, crucial aspects of individuals' collective experiences are insulated from democratic egalitarian reforms. It is, however, precisely these aspects of our lives that we need to take in charge, if we are to have any prospect of obtaining what egalitarians ultimately want.

Democratic Equality

Following Rousseau's lead, but extending and generalizing his notion of citizenship, I have suggested that democratic equality represents a very deep expression of democratic aspirations. I have also argued that democratic equality represents a better understanding of the requirements of equal respect for moral personality than liberal equality does—at least when equity and efficiency matter little because scarcity is largely overcome. Once scarcity is no longer an obstacle, there is no reason to insist, as a matter of justice, that persons not be indemnified for the untoward consequences of their own free choices. The presumption favoring strictly equal distributions would therefore be more difficult to overcome than in a society in which liberal egalitarian principles obtain. Ironically, then, just as the long-standing objective of egalitarian politics—the idea that everyone should have equal holdings of the right distribuand—would finally become unobjectionable, the distribution of things to persons would no longer express the egalitarian's deepest commitment to the moral equality of persons. Social citizenship would. Thus the egalitarian tradition culminates where a generalized Rousseauian model of democratic citizenship or the Marxian idea of communism begins. What would matter, for those concerned to make the moral equality of persons an earthly fact, is the equal distribution, to the greatest extent possible, of democratic rights over all significant aspects of collective life.

When democratic equality finally comes into its own, it will hardly matter who gets what. But it still does not follow that the presumption in favor of strictly equal distributions (of the right distribuand) will hold in all cases. I will conclude by reflecting briefly on some reasons why even democratic egalitarians might favor unequal distributions of things to persons. Neither equity nor efficiency considerations would warrant doing so. But the valuational commitments that motivate the extension of the Rousseauian model of citizenship to the economy and to society at large might.

Chief among these commitments is, of course, autonomy. I have tried to show that, despite what liberal egalitarians may suppose, support for autonomy does not in principle require holding individuals responsible for the distributional consequences of their free choices. With the subsidence of the circumstances of justice, autonomy considerations pose no obstacle in the way of strictly equal distributions. But the other values undergirding democratic equality, *republican community* and *Aristotelian self-realization,* are a different matter.

It is fair to speculate that, no matter how thoroughly human beings are transformed by democratic and liberal institutions, and no matter how affluent the societies in which they live become, republican communitarian concerns would still sometimes countervail the presumption favoring strictly equal distributions. To achieve outcome equality, it would be necessary to indemnify persons for virtually everything. But it is very likely that too much indemnification of flagrantly uncooperative individuals—for example, those who continually squander what they take from the common stock—would diminish communal solidarities severely. In communist conditions, restoring what wastrels have thrown away would cause no significant diminution in the well-being of others, nor would it adversely affect anyone else's distributive share—assuming, of course, that wastrels and other recalcitrants were few in number, relative to the vast majority of active, self-realizing citizens. The problem, therefore, has nothing to do with efficiency or justice. Nor is the situation similar to the refusal of liberal egalitarians to acknowledge the justice of a right not to work. It is not blindness to the implications of their own theoretical commitments that would lead communist men and women not to want to indemnify individuals who engage in gratuitously wasteful or reckless behavior. This attitude is a *normal*—and almost certainly universal—human response to an unhealthy situation. Unless social citizens were somehow to develop an unappealing tolerance for antisocial behavior, continually replenishing the holdings of willful squanderers would almost certainly undermine the cohesion of the community itself. It would be an irritant working against the background conditions that make an expanded Rousseauian citizenship possible. Even now, considerations of equity or efficiency hardly obtain within families. But family members who continually make good the losses that other family members incur through waste or negligence or recklessness put the cohesion of the family unit in jeopardy. A communist society that sought to promote outcome equality, come what may, would find itself in similar straits. It would be a dysfunctional family writ large.

It is also likely that a society that actively seeks to enhance its citizens' prospects for Aristotelian self-realization would want persons to bear at least some of the costs and reap some of the benefits of their own freely chosen activities. To this end, it might be expedient sometimes to have individuals' distributive shares depend to some degree on what these individuals freely choose to do. Thus at least some of the inequalities that liberal egalitarians would insist upon as a matter of justice might come back in—even in communist societies—for this very different reason. I would hazard that this concession to inequality is considerably less far-reaching than the liberal egalitarian's. But it is a concession nonetheless.

Thus it may be that the egalitarian's most long-standing aim—implementation of the principle "to each the same"—cannot be realized completely, even in the "utopian" conditions envisioned here. But from an egalitarian perspective, this is not an outcome to regret. In a regime of full democratic equality, what would then be blocking the fulfillment of this venerable objective would be the deepest goals of egalitarianism itself.

Existing theory supports only tentative and incomplete speculations about the nature of supraliberal societies. But even if there were a more developed theoretical arsenal to deploy, it would still be pointless to speculate about decisions undertaken by members of communities living in conditions vastly different from our own, and under institutional arrangements of which we can form only a vague idea. In reflecting on social ideals, as in chess, it is possible, at best, to see only a few moves ahead, and utterly impossible to envision how a game will end before play has even begun. Recent developments in liberal theory have put the idea of equality in the forefront of philosophical discussion. But until real-world politics catches up with and surpasses this philosophical representation of existing values and practices, the prospects for implementing anything more "utopian" are bleak indeed. For now, therefore, the task is to sustain a sense of the end in view, not to concoct what Marx called "recipes for the cookshops of the future." Egalitarians who, like myself, reprove the debilitating "realism" of contemporary political thinking can only applaud the revival of egalitarian theory that recent liberalism has launched—despite the manifest "antiutopianism" that distinguishes this strain of otherwise quite radical political philosophy. But we must also remain resolute in our determination to push this liberalism to its limits and beyond. However paradoxical it may be, the plain fact is that this body of doctrine, self-consciously dedicated to improving the status quo without altering its fundamental constitution, does point the way toward a cogent, desirable, and feasible "utopian" ideal.

Conclusion

Liberals who support the convictions that animate practicing egalitarians would probably agree that *if* the salience of the circumstances of justice receded significantly, the world would be different enough to warrant more (intuitively) egalitarian positions than liberal egalitarianism allows. Perhaps they would agree as well that what would follow is something like what I have gestured toward. But even if they are sympathetic to the case I have presented for democratic equality, I suspect that rather than sign on as supraliberal egalitarians, they would insist that my arguments can be incorporated into the prevailing liberal consensus. They could point out that I have largely agreed with them about how institutional arrangements ought to be organized in conditions where the circumstances of justice loom as large as they now do. Although I have been less celebratory than most self-described liberals about the democratic component of liberal democracy, liberals will maintain correctly that this difference hardly underwrites anything so portentous as a call to *transcend* liberalism itself. To go beyond liberalism, according to the arguments I have mustered, it is necessary to imagine a world of affluence, a world in which scarcity is no longer of overwhelming normative significance. I suggested that the maldistribution of existing wealth accounts, in part, for the widespread perception that scarcity remains a virulent fact of the human condition. I suspect that many liberals would agree with this contention, and also with the idea that actually existing scarcity is deeper and more pervasive than need be. Thus I imagine that some liberals might even concede that the demands of fairness should sometimes be relaxed for the sake of other fundamental liberal commitments, as I argued (in Chapter 1) in defense of a right not to work. But it is one thing to accept all of these positions and something else to declare scarcity surpassable (or, indeed, already largely surpassed) — to a degree that we can reasonably assume a vantage point *beyond* justice. Liberal egalitarianism's appeal, after all, is precisely its fit with prevailing views of what justice requires. Holding individuals responsible for the distributional consequences of their free choices, and for nothing else, is, liberal egalitarians contend, a fair way to distribute scarce resources. This argument is persuasive because fairness matters. On this apparently incontrovertible point, liberals can rest their case. Thus I expect that many readers will conclude that, my self-representations notwithstanding, I have not in fact presented an alternative to liberalism. I have only given a "utopian" spin to positions liberals already endorse. What I have done, they will say, is revive an idea of progress that has faded from liberal concerns. I have, of course, drawn on extraliberal theoretical resources — Rousseau's model of democratic citizenship and Marx's account of communism. But they will say that even so, I have not fundamentally challenged liberalism itself. At most, my arguments, if taken to heart, would only restore a view about humanity's prospects that liberal egalitarians, like almost everyone else in the final quarter of the twentieth century, have come to regard with skepticism. Many readers will then add that this skepticism is well founded and that the view of progress I have invoked is, at best, anachronistic.

Thus I expect that even sympathetic liberals will be tempted to describe the effort undertaken here as an example of the kind of political philosophy I claim to supersede. They will say that the differences between supraliberal theory, as I have sketched it, and the liberalism I claim it should replace derive entirely from different assessments of the prospects for changing the conditions under which political philosophers and political actors must operate. As for my claim that the circumstances of justice, though present from the beginnings of human civilization, are nevertheless transient features of the human condition, whereas the liberals I ostensibly oppose consider them permanent, they will say that for all practical purposes this is only a "theoretical" disagreement, and an unimportant one at that.

Less sympathetic readers will insist that my claims for the possibility of overcoming the circumstances of justice are unsubstantiated. They will therefore conclude that I have only colored existing views with an old-fashioned left-wing optimism that even left-wingers today no longer abide. These same readers might object as well that it is irresponsible to convey the impression that a supraliberal theory of the sort I have in mind is in any way practicable or even desirable. They will say that defending institutional arrangements that purport to transcend liberalism can only undermine the fragile liberal institutions on which we all depend. Political liberals especially will insist that in the present conjuncture the most urgent political task is to defend existing liberal gains and not, wittingly or not, to aid liberalism's enemies by promoting a vision that allegedly transcends the conditions that make liberalism necessary.

I have, in contrast, promoted a very different political posture, according to which a theoretically well-elaborated supraliberal end in view, communism (small *c*), is crucial for advancing even modest attempts at moving society closer to treating persons as moral equals. Without such a unifying vision of ideal social, political, and economic arrangements, the impulses that propelled the historical Left are unlikely to issue in anything more formidable than what we have today: a motley of well-intentioned efforts of very dubious efficacy that serve egalitarian aims poorly at best. I would venture, in fact, that in the present conjuncture the best way to defend liberal gains is to pursue positions beyond liberalism. But my reasons for advocating democratic over liberal equality have little directly to do with the political orientation I think it wisest to adopt. The differences between liberal and democratic equality and the larger social visions for which they are integral are not reducible to questions of emphasis or political spin.

To be sure, I have engaged liberalism politically, especially in making a case against political liberalism (in Chapter 3) and in putting liberal democracy in question (in Chapter 4). But my defense of democratic equality does not depend on considerations of this sort alone. Democratic equality is not a liberal egalitarian idea, and certainly not an anachronistic take on positions liberals already endorse. There is an irreducible philosophical difference between liberal and democratic equality, and therefore between liberal and supraliberal theory.

For liberals, as for contemporary political philosophers generally, equality has to do, in the first instance, with justice. This is why egalitarianism can be construed as a substantive principle of justice: "to each the same." So conceived, this principle supplies content to the formal principle that like cases should be treated alike. Historically, egalitarians have considered everyone to whom the formal principle applies a like case, and therefore wanted everyone to have equal—or rather equivalent—holdings (of the right distribuand). But as we have seen, it is misleading to collapse egalitarian concerns into the theory of distributive justice. Where the circumstances of justice obtain in full force, the commitment to respect the moral equality of persons devolves into a dedication to treat persons in the ways that liberal justice requires. As the circumstances of justice recede, however, the moral urgency of doing so diminishes correspondingly. But the need to respect the moral equality of persons, to implement deep equality, remains in force. Thus equality and justice part ways. My aim (especially in Chapters 4 and 5) has been to investigate what deep equality requires at a time when the salience of the circumstances of justice subsides. If economic development does indeed make (near) abundance materially possible, as I have suggested, it puts a qualitative transformation in the human condition on the agenda, with profound ramifications for moral philosophy and, of course, for the egalitarian project. It would then emerge that, contrary to what is almost universally assumed, there is no necessary connection between equality and justice. In conditions of (near) abundance, equality is not about justice at all.

Again, it may be useful to risk being obscure by expressing this idea in terms derived from Hegelian philosophy. By looking at equality, as best we can, from the standpoint of its "end," from how it appears after its internal logic has unfolded, we are able to gain a definitive purchase on what it really is. Thus we have seen that however much equality may have had to do with justice in the past, and however likely it is that this state of affairs will persist for an indefinite future, justice is not what equality is ultimately about. In the end, equality has to do with community or, more precisely, with the type of community implicit in Rousseau's account of democratic citizenship. Therefore what equality requires is not quite that individuals have equal distributive shares of the right distribuand (whatever it may be), even though it is likely, as we have seen, that some close approximation of this outcome will emerge as a by-product of the fullest possible implementation of egalitarian aims. What egalitarians want is not equal distribution per se, but the generalization of the model of citizenship Rousseau developed for the just state— beyond the political arena and into the economy and into society at large. Community so conceived, as we saw in Chapter 4, is integrally related to another idea, also endorsed at least implicitly by both liberals and democrats: self-realization. A community of social citizens is an association of autonomous individuals, drawn together to enable persons to become what they potentially are. As Marx said of communism, it is a social order in which "the free development of each [person] . . . [is] the condition for the free development of all." Of course, in describing communism this way, Marx had neither Rousseau nor egalitarianism in mind. Even so, Marxian communism corresponds, roughly, to Rousseau's notion of community—generalized and instantiated in what is arguably a historically realizable form. This is why Marx's scattered and under-elaborated reflections on communism provide the best available account of what egalitarians want.

Thus the case presented here for democratic equality is not just a liberal egalitarian argument delivered from an unreconstructed "utopian" vantage point. Democratic equality does "incorporate" liberal objectives. But it is a different concept. This is why my position is not reducible to the comparatively uncontroversial claim that liberal equality, for all its unexpected and radically redistributive implications, still sanctions deviations from strict outcome equality that can be relaxed as the circumstances of justice recede. This claim is true, but it is not the whole story or even the most important part of it. What I have tried to show instead is that, in the end, egalitarianism is not about distributive outcomes at all. For liberals, egalitarianism is a substantive principle of justice, neither more nor less. For supraliberals, it is much more. Ultimately, egalitarianism articulates a particular vision of ideal social arrangements. This vision is not only about the distribution of some distribuand. It is about communism (small *c*), the generalized form of Rousseauian citizenship. The "equality of what" debate therefore addresses only one aspect of what egalitarians want—an aspect of overwhelming importance in our time and place, but of virtually no importance in circumstances that, as Hegelians might say, are immanent in our present condition. In short, the "equality of what" writers consider the question they pose in a historically particular and ultimately inadequate way.

In the end, what egalitarians want is a democratic community of self-realizing, morally autonomous agents. This objective *explains* the liberal egalitarians' concern with the fairness of distributional outcomes. To the extent that justice matters, fairness is indispensable for building communities of the requisite sort. It is indispensable instrumentally because unfair treatment is bound to generate grievances, and aggrieved individuals will not form together into republican communities. It is also indispensable intrinsically. As we have seen (mainly in Chapter 2), in conditions of scarcity a commitment to deep equality mandates fair treatment by basic social institutions. But scarcity is (mostly) eliminable. Therefore fairness, as liberal egalitarians understand it, is not *timelessly* urgent. To wax Hegelian for a final time, the concerns evinced by the "equality of what" writers speak to a "moment" in the unfolding of equality's "becoming," an episode that real history will be able in principle eventually to surpass.

As it has developed historically, liberalism presumes the centrality of justice. Thus it is entirely true to its spirit that Rawls, the preeminent liberal philosopher of the past quarter-century, accords justice a preeminent role in the assessment of basic social, political, and economic institutions. In doing so, Rawls represents a morally important fact about the situation we confront. But this concern is parochial nevertheless.

Ironically, there is a sense in which political liberals should be able to support this conclusion. Of course, they would not represent their views in quite so historicist a way, and they certainly do not envision a world *beyond* liberalism. But they eschew any ambition for political philosophy beyond merely giving expression to ideas latent in the dispositions and comprehensive doctrines of historically situated persons. Thus they should agree with my depiction of liberal egalitarianism's historical particularity. Political liberals then make a virtue of this fact, going on to contend, not altogether consistently, that liberalism, once achieved, is a political philosophy for all subsequent times and places. My aim has been to dispel this notion—and to restore to the philosophical imagination a deeper vision of the values that liberalism promotes.

Rethinking liberal equality is key in this endeavor because liberal egalitarianism perspicuously reveals liberalism's valuational commitments and also its limitations in realizing its aims. In Chapter 2, I raised the question of the connection between liberalism as a political philosophy and liberal egalitarianism. In the chapters that followed I suggested that the connection is mainly historical. I also suggested that at a more conceptual level the connection, such as it is, depends upon the preeminence both dimensions of (self-described) liberal theory accord to the idea of autonomy. We also saw, however, that this valuational commitment is hardly unique to liberalism; therefore this explanation will take us only so far. We can now add another consideration that may help to explain why the designation "liberal" seems apt in both contexts. Liberal political philosophy and liberal egalitarianism both express an underlying commitment to implementing deep equality in a historical period of an indefinitely long but not permanent duration—in which both are appropriate in their respective spheres of applicability and in which they are mutually reinforcing and complementary. This shared historical particularity (partly) explains their affinity. It also explains their limitations in giving theoretical and practical expression to what egalitarians ultimately want.

What, then, do egalitarians want? At present, only vague intimations of an answer are within reach. But we do know enough to conclude that the answer is not what liberal egalitarians think it is. Ultimately, what egalitarians want is democratic equality, a notion that must, for now, remain only barely elaborated. It is plain, even so, that the concept presupposes the subsidence of scarcity and the emergence of the social citizen. To defend democratic equality, therefore, it is necessary to assume the possibility of fundamental changes in the human condition and in human nature itself. Nowadays, as the very idea of radical change has fallen into disrepute, most erstwhile egalitarians have lost faith in this prospect. In a curious and ironic turn of events, it has fallen to liberal academics, hostile to "utopian" yearnings of any kind and at some considerable remove from real-world egalitarian political movements, to rescue egalitarian thinking from the oblivion into which the larger political culture would consign it. I have tried to show that egalitarians ought to take on board theoretical advances emanating from this quarter but ought not remain stalled where liberal egalitarianism leaves off. By assuming this stance they can advance philosophical understanding. But of far greater importance to anyone who would identify with the egalitarian tradition, rethinking liberal equality from a "utopian" point of view is indispensable for advancing the egalitarian project itself—and perhaps eventually, as conditions change, for seeing it through to its completion.

Bibliography

Ackerman, Bruce A. 1980. *Social Justice in the Liberal State.* New Haven: Yale University Press.

———. 1988. "Neo-Federalism?" In *Constitutionalism and Democracy,* edited by Jon Elster and Rune Slagstad. Cambridge: Cambridge University Press.

———. 1989. "Why Dialogue." *Journal of Philosophy* 86:5–22.

———. 1994. "Political Liberalisms." *Journal of Philosophy* 91, no. 7:364–86.

Arneson, Richard. 1989. "Equality and Equality of Opportunity for Welfare." *Philosophical Review* 56:77–93.

———. 1990. "Is Work Special? Justice and the Distribution of Employment and Job Satisfaction." *American Political Science Review* 88:1127–47.

Arrow, Kenneth. 1963. *Social Choice and Individual Values.* 2d ed. New York: John Wiley and Sons.

Augustine, St. 1950. *The City of God.* New York: Random House.

Baker, John. 1987. *Arguing for Equality.* London: Verso.

Balibar, Etienne, 1994. *Masses, Classes, Ideas: Studies on Politics and Philosophy before and after Marx.* New York: Routledge.

Barber, Benjamin. 1984. *Strong Democracy: Participatory Politics for a New Age.* Berkeley: University of California Press.

Baumol, William J. 1965. *Welfare Economics and the Theory of the State.* 2d ed. Cambridge: Harvard University Press.

Berlin, Isaiah. 1969. *Four Essays on Liberty.* Oxford: Oxford University Press.

Block, Fred. 1990. *Post-industrial Possibilities: A Critique of Economic Discourse.* Berkeley: University of California Press.

Bowles, Samuel, and Herbert Gintis, eds. 1998. *Recasting Egalitarianism: New Rules for Communities, States, and Markets.* London: Verso.

Brighouse, Harry. 1996. "Egalitarianism and Equal Availability of Political Influence." *Journal of Political Philosophy* 4:118–41.

Broad, C. D. 1916. "On the Function of False Hypotheses in Ethics." *International Journal of Ethics* 26:384–90.

Burnheim, John. 1985. *Is Democracy Possible?* Berkeley: University of California Press.

Cohen, G. A. 1978. *Karl Marx's Theory of History: A Defence.* Oxford: Oxford University Press; Princeton: Princeton University Press.

——. 1989. "On the Currency of Egalitarian Justice." *Ethics* 99:906–44.

——. 1991. "Incentives, Inequality and Community." In *The Tanner Lectures on Human Values.* Salt Lake City: University of Utah Press. Reprinted in Darwall 1995, 331–97.

Cohen, Joshua. 1990. "Moral Pluralism and Political Consensus." In Copp, Hampton, and Roemer 1993.

Cole, G. D. H. 1944. *Money: Its Present and Future.* London: Fabian.

Copp, David, Jean Hampton, and John Roemer, eds. 1993. *The Idea of Democracy.* Cambridge: Cambridge University Press.

Cullity, Garett. 1995. "Moral Free Riding." *Philosophy and Public Affairs* 24, no. 1:3–34.

Daniels, Normal. 1975. *Reading Rawls.* New York: Basic Books.

Darwall, Stephen, ed. 1995. *Equal Freedom: Selected Tanner Lectures on Human Values.* Ann Arbor: University of Michigan Press.

Dasgupta, Partha. 1993. *An Inquiry into Well-Being and Destitution.* Oxford: Oxford University Press.

Debreu, Gerard. 1959. *Theory of Value: An Axiomatic Analysis of Economic Equilibrium.* New York: Wiley.

De Grazia, Sebastian. 1962. *Of Time, Work and Leisure.* New York: Twentieth Century Fund.

De Jasay, Anthony. 1989. *Social Contract, Free Ride.* Oxford: Oxford University Press.

Dewey, John. 1979. *Democracy and Education.* In *The Middle Works of John Dewey: 1899–1924,* vol. 9. Carbondale: Southern Illinois University Press.

Dworkin, Ronald. 1978. "Liberalism." In *Public and Private Morality,* edited by Stuart Hampshire. Cambridge: Cambridge University Press.

——. 1981a. "What is Equality? Part 1: Equality of Welfare," *Philosophy and Public Affairs* 10:283–345.

——. 1981b. "What Is Equality? Part 2: Equality of Resources." *Philosophy and Public Affairs* 10:655–69.

——. 1987. "What is Equality? Part 4: Political Equality." *University of San Francisco Law Review* 22, no. 1:1–30.

——. 1988. "Foundations of Liberal Equality." *Tanner Lectures.* Reprinted in Darwall 1995, 190–306.

Elster, Jon. 1979. *Ulysses and the Sirens: Studies in Rationality and Irrationality.* Cambridge: Cambridge University Press; Paris: Editions de la Maison des Sciences de l'Homme.

——. 1983. *Sour Grapes: Studies in the Subversion of Rationality.* Cambridge: Cambridge University Press; Paris: Editions de la Maison des Sciences de l'Homme.

——. 1988. "Is There (or Should There Be) a Right to Work?" In *Democracy and the Welfare State,* edited by Amy Gutman. Princeton: Princeton University Press.

——. 1989a. *Solomonic Judgments.* Cambridge: Cambridge University Press.

——. 1989b. "Self-Realization in Work and Politics." In Elster and Moene 1989, 127–58.

Elster, Jon, and Karl Ove Moene. 1989. *Alternatives to Capitalism.* Cambridge: Cambridge University Press.

Elster, Jon, and Rune Slagstad. 1988. *Constitutionalism and Democracy.* Cambridge: Cambridge University Press.

Estlund, David. 1996. "The Survival of Egalitarian Justice in John Rawls's *Political Liberalism. Journal of Political Philosophy* 4:68–78.

Fralin, Richard. 1978. *Rousseau and Representation: A Study in the Development of His Concept of Political Institutions.* New York: Cambridge University Press.

Freud, Sigmund. 1927. *The Future of an Illusion.* In *The Standard Edition of the Complete Psychological Works of Sigmund Freud,* edited by James Strachy, vol. 21. London: Hogarth Press.

Friedman, Milton. 1962. *Capitalism and Freedom.* Chicago: University of Chicago Press.

Galston, William A. 1995. "Two Concepts of Liberalism." *Ethics* 105:516–34.

Gilbert, Alan. 1990. *Democratic Individuality.* Cambridge: Cambridge University Press.

Goodin, Robert. 1988. *Reasons for Welfare: The Political theory of the Welfare State.* Princeton: Princeton University Press.

——. 1992. "Towards a Minimally Presumptuous Social Welfare Policy." In *Arguing for Basic Income,* edited by Philippe Van Parijs. London: Verso.

Gordon, Linda. 1994. *Pitied But Not Entitled.* New York: Free Press.

Gorz, André. 1989. *Critique of Economic Reason.* London: Verso.

Greenawalt, Kent. 1988. *Religious Convictions and Political Choice.* Oxford: Oxford University Press.

Gutmann, Amy. 1985. "Communitarian Critics of Liberalism." *Philosophy and Public Affairs* 14:308–22.

——. 1993. "The Challenge of Multiculturalism in Political Ethics." *Philosophy and Public Affairs* 22:171–206.

Habermas, Jürgen. 1995. "Reconciliation through the Public Use of Reason: Remarks on John Rawls' Political Liberalism." *Journal of Philosophy* 92, no. 3:109–31.

Hardin, Russell. 1989. *Morality within the Limits of Reason.* Chicago: University of Chicago Press.

Hart, Herbert L. A. 1955. "Are There Any Natural Rights?" *Philosophical Review* 64:175–91.

——. 1961. *The Concept of Law.* Oxford: Clarendon Press.

Hegel, G. W. F. 1807. *The Phenomenology of Mind.* Edited and Translated by J. B. Baillie. London: George Allen and Unwin.

Hobbes, Thomas. 1651. *Leviathan.* Edited by Michael Oakeshott. Oxford: Basil Blackwell.

Hobsbawm, Eric. 1994. *The Age of Extremes: A History of the World, 1914–1991.* New York: Pantheon.

Holmes, Stephen. 1995. *Passions and Constraint: On the Theory of Liberal Democracy.* Chicago: University of Chicago Press.

Hume, David. 1896. *A Treatise of Human Nature.* Edited by L. A. Selby Bigge. Oxford: Oxford University Press.

——. 1977. *An Enquiry Concerning the Principles of Morals.* Edited by Eric Steinberg. Indianapolis: Hackett.

Kafka, Franz. 1946. *Parables and Paradoxes.* New York: Schocken Books.

Kant, Immanuel. 1959. *Foundations of the Metaphysics of Morals.* 1785. Reprint, New York: Library of Liberal Arts.

Kolakowski, Leszek. 1978. *Main Currents of Marxism.* 3 vols. Oxford: Clarendon Press.

Kornai, Janos. 1992. *The Socialist System: The Political Economy of Communism.* Princeton: Princeton University Press.

Kuhn, Thomas S. 1962. *The Structure of Scientific Revolutions* Chicago: University of Chicago Press.

Kymlicka, Will. 1989. *Liberalism, Community and Culture.* Oxford: Clarendon Press.

———. 1995. *Multi-Cultural Citizenship: A Liberal Theory of Minority Rights.* Oxford: Oxford University Press.

Lange, Oscar. 1936–37. "On the Economic Theory of Socialism." *Review of Economic Studies* 4:53–71, 123–42.

Lange, Oscar, and Fred M. Taylor. 1938. *On the Economic Theory of Socialism.* Edited by Benjamin Lippincott. Minneapolis: University of Minnesota Press.

Larmore, Charles. 1987. *Patterns of Moral Complexity.* Cambridge: Cambridge University Press.

Levine, Andrew. 1976. *The Politics of Autonomy: A Kantian Reading of Rousseau's "Social Contract."* Amherst: University of Massachusetts Press.

———. 1981. *Liberal Democracy: A Critique of Its Theory.* New York: Columbia University Press.

———. 1987. *The End of the State.* London: Verso.

———. 1988. *Arguing for Socialism: Theoretical Considerations.* 2d ed. London: Verso.

———. 1993. *The General Will: Rousseau, Marx, Communism.* Cambridge: Cambridge University Press.

———. 1996. "Saving Socialism and/or Abandoning It." In *Real Utopias,* edited by E. O. Wright, vol. 2. London: Verso.

———. 1998. "Efficiency: What? Which? Why? and When?" In Bowles and Gintis 1998.

Lindbloom, Charles E. 1977. *Politics and Markets: The World's Political-Economic Systems.* New York: Basic Books.

Little, I. M. D. 1957. *A Critique of Welfare Economics.* 2d ed. Oxford: Oxford University Press, 1957.

Locke, John. 1980. *Second Treatise of Government.* Edited by C. B. Macpherson. 1690. Reprint, Indianapolis: Hackett.

Lucas, J. R. 1966. *The Principles of Politics.* Oxford: Clarendon Press.

Lukes, Steven. 1995. *The Curious Enlightenment of Professor Caritat.* London: Verso.

MacCallum, Gerald. 1967. "Negative and Positive Freedom." *Philosophical Review* 76, no. 3:312–34.

MacIntyre, Alasdair. 1981. *After Virtue.* Notre Dame: Notre Dame University Press.

Macpherson, C. B. 1973. *Democratic Theory: Essays in Retrieval.* Oxford: Clarendon Press.

Malthus, Thomas R. 1958. *Essay on the Principle of Population,* 2 vols. 1798. Reprint, London: J. M. Dent and Sons.

Marcuse, Herbert, Barrington Moore, Jr., and Robert Paul Wolff. 1965. *A Critique of Pure Tolerance.* Boston: Beacon.

Marx, Karl, and Friedrich Engels. 1962. *Selected Works in Two Volumes.* Moscow: Foreign Languages Publishing House.

———. 1964. *Early Writings.* Edited by T. B. Bottomore. New York: Mc-Graw Hill.

———. 1965. *Capital.* Vol. 1. Moscow: Progress Publishers.

Mill, John Stuart. 1950. *Considerations on Representative Government.* 1861. Reprint, New York: E. P. Dutton.

———. 1956. *On Liberty.* Edited by Curtin V. Shields. 1859. Reprint, New York: Bobbs-Merrill.

Moon, J. Donald. 1988. "The Moral Basis of the Democratic Welfare State." In *Democracy and the Welfare State,* edited by Amy Gutmann. Princeton: Princeton University Press.

Musgrave, Richard. 1974. "Maximin, Uncertainty and the Leisure Trade-Off." *Quarterly Journal of Economics* 88:625–32.

Nagel, Thomas. 1987. "Moral Conflict and Political Legitimacy." *Philosophy and Public Affairs* 16:215–40.

Nedelsky, Jennifer. 1989. "Reconceiving Autonomy." *Yale Journal of Law and Feminism* 1:7–35.

Nietzsche, Friedrick. 1974. *The Gay Science.* Edited and translated by Walter Kaufmann. New York: Random House.

Nozick, Robert. 1974. *Anarchy, State, Utopia.* New York: Basic Books.

Okin, Susan Moller. 1989. *Justice, Gender and the Family.* New York: Basic Books.

Pateman, Carole. 1970. *Participation and Democratic Theory.* Cambridge: Cambridge University Press.

Perelman, Chaim. 1963. *The Idea of Justice and the Problem of Argument.* Translated by John Petrie. New York: Humanities Press.

Pettit, Philip. 1997. *Republicanism: A Theory of Freedom and Government.* Oxford: Oxford University Press.

Pippin, Robert B. 1991. *Modernism as a Philosophical Problem: On the Dissatisfactions of European High Culture.* Oxford: Blackwell.

Pogge, Thomas W. 1989. *Realizing Rawls.* Ithaca: Cornell University Press.

Przeworski, Adam. 1991. *Democracy and the Market: Political and Economic Reforms in Eastern Europe and Latin America.* Cambridge: Cambridge University Press.

Rawls, John. 1971. *A Theory of Justice.* Cambridge: Harvard University Press.

——. 1974. "Reply to Alexander and Musgrave." *Quarterly Journal of Economics* 88:633–55.

——. 1975. "Fairness to Goodness." *Philosophical Review,* 84:536–54.

——. 1982. "Social Unity and Primary Goods." In *Utilitarianism and Beyond,* edited by Amartya Sen and Bernard Williams, 159–85. Cambridge: Cambridge University Press.

——. 1985. "Justice as Fairness: Political Not Metaphysical." *Philosophy and Public Affairs* 14:223–51.

——. 1987. "The Idea of an Overlapping Consensus." *Oxford Legal Studies* 1:1–25.

——. 1988. "The Priority of Right and Ideas of the Good." *Philosophy and Public Affairs* 17:251–76.

——. 1989. "The Domain of the Political and Overlapping Consensus." *New York University Law Review* 2:233–55.

——. 1993. *Political Liberalism.* New York: Columbia University Press.

——. 1995. "Reply to Habermas." *Journal of Philosophy* 92:132–80.

Raz, Joseph. 1990. "Facing Diversity: The Case of Epistemic Abstinence." *Philosophy and Public Affairs* 19:3–46.

Redish, Martin. 1982. "The Value of Free Speech." *University of Pennsylvania Law Review* 91:591–645.

Reiss, Hans, ed. 1970. *Kant's Political Writings.* Cambridge: Cambridge University Press.

Roemer, John. 1981. *Analytical Foundations of Marxian Economic Theory.* Cambridge: Cambridge University Press.

——. 1982a. *A General Theory of Exploitation and Class.* Cambridge: Harvard University Press.

——. 1982b. "New Directions in the Marxian Theory of Exploitation and Class." *Politics and Society* 11:253–87. Reprinted in *Analytical Marxism,* edited by J. E. Roemer, 81–113. Cambridge: Cambridge University Press, 1986.

——. 1982c. "Reply." *Politics and Society* 11:281–83.

——. 1983. "Are Socialist Ethics Consistent with Efficiency?" *Philosophical Forum* 14:369–88.

——. 1985a. "Should Marxists Be Interested in Exploitation?" *Philosophy and Public Affairs* 14:30–65. Reprinted in *Analytical Marxism,* edited by J. E. Roemer, 260–82. Cambridge: Cambridge University Press, 1986.

——. 1985b. "Equality of Talent." *Economics and Philosophy* 1:151–87.

——. 1986. "Equality of Resources Implies Equality of Welfare." *Quarterly Journal of Economics* 101:751–84.

——. 1988. *Free to Lose.* Cambridge: Harvard University Press.

——. 1994. *A Future for Socialism.* Cambridge: Harvard University Press.

——. 1995. "An Anti-Hayekian Manifesto." *New Left Review* 211:112–30.

Rousseau, Jean Jacques. 1983. *The Social Contract.* 1762. Reprint, Indianapolis: Hackett.

Sahlins, Marshal. 1972. *Stone Age Economics.* New York: Aldine.

Sandel, Michael. 1982. *Liberalism and the Limits of Justice.* Cambridge: Cambridge University Press.

Satz, Debra. 1992. "Markets in Women's Reproductive Labor." *Philosophy and Public Affairs* 21:107–31.

——. 1995. "Markets in Women's Sexual Labor." *Ethics* 106:63–85.

Scanlon, Thomas. 1972. "A Theory of Free Expression." *Philosophy and Public Affairs* 1:204–29.

——. 1982. "Contractualism and Utilitarianism." In *Utilitarianism and Beyond,* edited by Amartya Sen and Bernard Williams, 103–28. Cambridge: Cambridge University Press.

——. 1986. "The Significance of Choice." *Tanner Lectures.* Reprinted in Darwall 1995, 39–104.

——. 1991. "The Moral Basis of Interpersonal Comparisons." In *Interpersonal Comparisons of Well-Being,* edited by Jon Elster and John E. Roemer. Cambridge: Cambridge University Press.

Schor, Juliet B. 1991. *The Overworked American: The Unexpected Decline of Leisure.* New York: Basic Books.

Schumpeter, Joseph A. 1942. *Capitalism, Socialism and Democracy.* New York: Harper and Row.

Schweickart, David. 1980. *Capitalism or Worker Control? An Ethical and Economic Appraisal.* New York: Praeger.

——. 1996. *Against Capitalism.* Boulder, Colorado: Westview.

Sen, Amartya K. 1980. "Equality of What?" In *The Tanner Lectures on Human Values,* vol. 1, edited by S. M. McMurrin. Salt Lake City: University of Utah Press; Cambridge: Cambridge University Press.

——. 1992. *Inequality Reexamined.* New York: Russell Sage Foundation and Cambridge: Harvard University Press.

Shaw, George Bernard. 1928. *The Intelligent Woman's Guide to Socialism and Capitalism.* New York: Brentano.

Simmons, A. John. 1979. *Moral Principles and Political Obligations.* Princeton: Princeton University Press.

Smith, Adam. 1937. *The Wealth of Nations.* 1776. Reprint, New York: Random House.

Solum, Lawrence B. 1994. "Inclusive Public Reason." *Pacific Philosophical Quarterly* 75:217–31.

Stiglitz, Joseph E. 1994. *Whither Socialism?* Cambridge: MIT Press.

Strauss, David. 1991. "Persuasion, Autonomy and Freedom of Expression." *Columbia Law Review* 91:334–67.

Sunstein, Cass R. 1988. "Constitutions and Democracies." In *Constitutionalism and Democracy*, edited by Jon Elster and Rune Slagstad. Cambridge: Cambridge University Press.

Tawney, R. H. 1931. *Equality*. New York: Capricorn Books.

Taylor, Michael. 1987. *The Possibility of Cooperation*. Cambridge: Cambridge University Press.

Unger, Roberto Mangabeira. 1975. *Knowledge and Politics*. New York: Free Press.

Van Parijs, Philippe. 1991. "Why Surfers Should Be Fed: The Liberal Case for an Unconditional Basic Income." *Philosophy and Public Affairs* 20:101–31.

———. 1992a. "Basic Income Capitalism." *Ethics* 102:465–84.

———. 1992b. *Arguing for Basic Income*. London: Verso.

———. 1993. *Marxism Recycled*. Cambridge: Cambridge University Press.

———. 1995. *Real Freedom for All: What (If Anything) Can Justify Capitalism?* Oxford: Clarendon Press.

———. 1996. "Justice and Democracy: Are They Incompatible?" *Journal of Political Philosophy* 4:101–17.

Veyne, Paul. 1988. *Did the Greeks Believe in their Myths?: An Essay on the Constitutive Imagination*. Translated by Paula Wissing. Chicago: University of Chicago Press.

Waldron, Jeremy. 1993. "Justice Revisited." *Times Literary Supplement* 4707:5–6.

———. 1994. "Disagreements About Justice." *Pacific Philosophical Quarterly* 75:372–87.

Walter, Tony. 1989. *Basic Income: Freedom from Poverty, Freedom from Work*. London: Boyars.

Webb, Steven. 1990. *Beyond the Welfare State: An Examination of Basic Incomes in a Market Economy*. Aberdeen: Aberdeen University Press.

Weber, Max. 1958. "Politics as a Vocation." In *From Max Weber: Essays in Sociology*, edited by H. H. Gerth and C. Wright Mills. New York: Oxford University Press.

Weinstock, Daniel M. 1994. "The Justification of Political Liberalism." *Pacific Philosophical Quarterly* 75:163–85.

Weithman, Paul J. 1994. "Taking Rites Seriously." *Pacific Philosophical Quarterly* 75:272–94.

Williams, Bernard. 1962. "The Idea of Equality." In *Philosophy, Politics and Society*, 2d ser., edited by P. Laslett and W. G. Runciman, 110–31. New York: Barnes and Noble.

Wolff, Robert Paul. 1968. *The Poverty of Liberalism*. Boston: Beacon.

Wright, Erik Olin, Andrew Levine, and Elliott Sober. 1992. *Reconstructing Marxism*. London: Verso.

Index